## WARD LOC

### FAMILY HEALTH GUI

# MIGRAIN

# WARD LOCK

## FAMILY HEALTH GUIDE

# MIGRAINE

## RICKI OSTROV

WARD LOCK

A WARD LOCK BOOK

First published in the UK 1997
by Ward Lock
Wellington House
125 Strand
London
WC2R OBB

A Cassell Imprint

Distributed in Canada
by Cavendish Books Inc.
Unit 5, 801 West 1st Street
North Vancouver, BC V7B 1PH

A British Library Cataloguing in Publication Data block for this book may be obtained
from the British Library.

ISBN 0 7063 7528 9
Designed by Lindsey Johns at The Design Revolution, Brighton
Typeset by Central Southern Typesetting, Eastbourne
Printed and bound in Spain

**Acknowledgements**
Photographs on the following pages are reproduced by courtesy of Life File:
2 (Tim Fisher); 9, 21, 33, 42, 46, 67 (Emma Lee); 11, 28 (Andrew Ward);
14 (Jeremy Hoare); 16, 18, 77 (Ron Gregory); 30 (Angela Maynard);
37, 50, 54, 74 (Nicola Sutton); 40, 61 (Dave Thompson); 44, 47 (Mark Hibbert);
48 (L. J. Hall); 55 (Mike Evans); 70 (Terry O'Brien); 76 (Juliet Highet).

Cover photograph: Zefa Pictures.

# Contents

# Introduction

Migraine has been around for thousands of years. The earliest known record, which dates from around 3,500 years ago, was made by an ancient Egyptian courtesan. She described a one-sided headache that was accompanied by vomiting and lethargy. It was even thought that migraine was due to evil spirits within the head. Then, around 400 BC in ancient Greece, Hippocrates distinguished different types of headache, including migraine with aura. Indeed the word migraine derives from the Greek *hemicrania*, meaning 'half skull'. The first record we have of 'mygraine' in English dates from 1398, and although more became known about the condition, it was not until the second half of the twentieth century that this better understanding led to improved treatments.

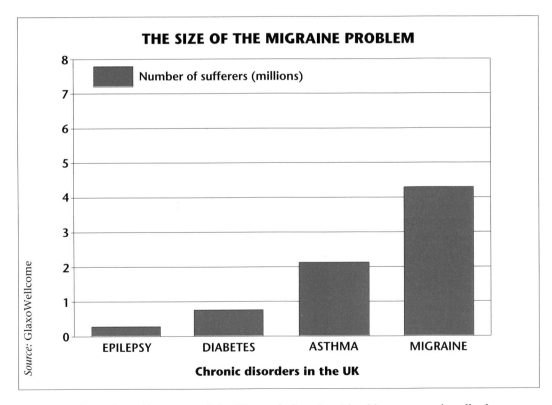

THE SIZE OF THE MIGRAINE PROBLEM

Number of sufferers (millions)

*Source:* GlaxoWellcome

EPILEPSY    DIABETES    ASTHMA    MIGRAINE

**Chronic disorders in the UK**

*Migraine affects about 10 per cent of the UK population. Considerably more people suffer from migraine than from many other chronic conditions including asthma, diabetes and epilepsy.*

Today migraine is estimated to affect about 10 per cent of the population in most developed countries. It is one of the most common chronic disorders – many more people suffer from migraine than from asthma, diabetes or epilepsy – and can strike anyone, including children and the elderly.

There is little doubt that migraine can have an almost immeasurable impact on sufferers' lives. Some studies have shown that the average sufferer experiences about one attack a month, with the average length of an attack being about a day. But many people suffer much more frequent and considerably longer attacks. All this time out of action means that the average sufferer has to take seven to ten days off work each year just as a result of migraine, costing business millions if not billions of pounds.

And what about the effect on sufferers themselves, as well as on their families and friends? A number try to struggle on through an attack for fear of letting others down or even losing their jobs. They may find that their condition has a harmful effect on their personal life – one study showed that it interfered with their physical relationship with their partner; and about 38 per cent of migraine sufferers had their condition on their mind almost constantly.

In spite of the huge scale of the problem, the vast majority of migraine sufferers do not ask their doctor for help. In some cases it could be that the attacks are very infrequent or not severe, or that sufferers are able to manage them well on their own. However, others may suspect that, because migraine is not life-threatening, it is not something to 'bother' the doctor about. Many people have become so used to living with their migraine they feel that there is little to be done. This is definitely not the case.

This book aims to explain what a migraine is, the different types of migraine, how a migraine develops and how to recognize the common signs and symptoms. It explains how to identify possible trigger factors and how to tackle them, in the hope that you may be able to reduce your attacks. It also discusses what lifestyle factors may be contributing to your condition, and how you can make some simple changes that may lessen your attacks. Knowing about migraine is important, as the more you understand about it, the better you will be able to manage.

Although there is, as yet, no cure for migraine, and there are still many unanswered questions about the cause and mechanism of this debilitating condition, there is also a wide variety of help available. Treatments can range from simple painkillers you buy at the pharmacy to strong prescription drugs to complementary therapies.

Once you realize how much is on offer, you will be able to decide which treatment(s) might be suitable for you. Then you will well and truly be on the road to controlling your migraines instead of having your migraines control you.

**Ricki Ostrov**

*Chapter one*

# What is migraine?

Headache is one of the most common symptoms known to the human race. Few of us can claim never to have had a headache, and it is estimated that around 90–95 per cent of people have suffered at one time or another. But all headaches are not created equal. There are different types of headache, some much more painful and debilitating than others. And one of the most difficult to control and to understand is the migraine headache.

Specialists who study headaches often define them according to their different causes.

● **Vascular headaches** are so called because they are thought to involve abnormal function of the brain's blood vessels, or vascular system. This group includes migraine headache.

● **Tension headaches** are usually caused by some type of physical or muscular tension, often around the neck and shoulders. They can also be due to environmental tension, such as stress and anxiety.

● **Inflammatory headaches** are usually caused by some area of inflammation elsewhere in the body – for example, a sinus headache.

## *How migraine is different*

Although many people assume that a migraine is just a severe headache, this is not the case at all. First migraine, unlike other headaches, lasts for quite a long time. It is generally accepted that a migraine can last anywhere from four to 72 hours. It does not occur on a daily basis, and when the migraine goes away, you are completely free from symptoms between attacks.

The headache that accompanies migraine is characterized by severe pain on one side of the head, though it can affect both sides. In addition there are other symptoms, most commonly vomiting or nausea, a dislike of noise or bright lights, and at times disturbed vision. The headache itself usually disappears within a day or so, but may last longer. And many sufferers have after effects, similar to a hangover, when the migraine has lifted. They may need another day or so to get back to feeling normal again.

The specific symptoms that develop will depend on the type of migraine you suffer. Some attacks – called classical migraine – are preceded by what is known as an aura: a period of about 20 to 30 minutes before the migraine

**8**

*The average sufferer has to take seven to ten days off work each year because of migraine attacks.*

attack begins when you may notice various symptoms, the most common being visual disturbances, such as flashing lights.

The frequency of migraine attacks can also vary considerably, both between individual sufferers and from attack to attack in the same person. You may find that you get attacks once or twice a month or even more often during a bad patch, and then have an attack-free period lasting for several months or years.

## The symptoms of migraine

As has been stated, suffering a migraine attack is not simply a matter of having a bad headache. It is the accompanying signs and symptoms that set migraine apart from an 'ordinary' headache.

# What is migraine?

## Warning signs

First there is often a warning period that a migraine is going to begin. This is called the prodromal phase (see page 13). You may find that you are yawning or lethargic, you notice changes in your mood or behaviour, or feel tired and irritable. Some sufferers feel almost as if they are on a 'high', while others have a depressed and low mood. Some people find they are cold or have a stiff neck, a craving for food, especially sweet or starchy foods, or fluid retention. You may also notice that you feel fuzzy-headed, and are unable to think clearly.

## The aura

The aura occurs only in classical migraine (see pages 20–1) and is experienced just before the headache. During an aura the most common complaint from migraine sufferers is that they have visual disturbances. You may notice flashing lights or stars and sparks, or even patterns in front of your eyes, though a huge variety of visual disturbances is reported. The most typical of these is a series of expanding zigzag lines across the field of vision. Some sufferers describe rippling or shimmering vision, while others complain of a blind spot, temporarily losing part of their vision in only one area. The visual disturbances were thought to be caused by reduced blood flow to the occipital lobes, the area in the back of the brain that affects and controls vision. This is no longer believed to be the case and the true cause remains unclear.

It is not only your vision that can be affected during an aura. Neurological symptoms may occur occasionally. Most frequently these are a sensation of pins and needles, or tingling and numbness, that can gradually spread up from your fingers and hand to the face over a period of around 15 to 20 minutes. You may find that your speech is slurred, you have double vision and are unsteady on your feet. As with the visual aura, these symptoms gradually disappear as the headache begins to develop.

An aura can be very frightening, especially the first few times you get a migraine. Initially you may not know what is happening to you, and you may suspect you have a brain tumour or a stroke. But with migraine the symptoms will gradually build up and gradually disappear, especially as the headache comes on. However, if any of these symptoms lasts for more than an hour, you should contact your doctor. They may, in fact, not be caused by migraine but by some other condition that needs treatment.

## The headache

Some people describe a migraine headache as being the worst you can imagine. In most instances the headache is on one side only. However, some people do suffer pain on both sides of the head. And the side can vary within an attack as well as from attack to attack. For instance, some people who normally have the headache on their right side will suffer left-sided headaches occasionally, and *vice versa*.

The pain of a migraine headache is usually in the forehead or temples, but it can also start from the back of the neck. It is often initially described as a throbbing or pulsating sensation, but as it worsens it can feel as if your head is bursting. Some people find they wake up with the headache first thing in the morning.

*The pain of migraine is usually made worse by any movement, even as gentle an activity as washing up.*

The pain may grow stronger as your attack progresses, and it is usually made worse when you move around, or by any movement, including coughing or sneezing. This is why so many sufferers find that they need to lie still during an attack.

## Digestive disturbances

Another common feature of migraine is digestive disturbances. These usually occur at the same time you have the headache, though occasionally they can also develop during the warning phase of a migraine.

Nausea is by far the most common digestive trouble, and it is suspected to occur in around 95 per cent of migraine attacks. It can be so severe that the smell – or even the thought – of food can make you feel ill. In fact many sufferers lose their appetite altogether during a migraine. In some people the smell of scents or cigarettes, which they normally like or at least find inoffensive, can bring on a feeling of nausea at this time.

Vomiting occurs in about a quarter of all migraine attacks, and seems to be more common in children who suffer from migraine than in adults. At times the vomiting may be so severe that you cannot even keep water or migraine medication down. And it is during the headache that the nausea, vomiting or other digestive symptoms occur.

## Photophobia

Dislike of bright lights, which is called photophobia, occurs in about 80 per cent of attacks, whether the migraine is with or without an aura. This symptom usually develops at around the time when the headache is experienced. This is often why many sufferers prefer to lie in a darkened room – they find that exposure to light makes their headache much worse.

## Phonophobia

A dislike of noise, known as phonophobia, is another common symptom of migraine. The noise does not need to be loud. Again it usually occurs at the same time as the headache and often makes the pain worse.

# What is migraine?

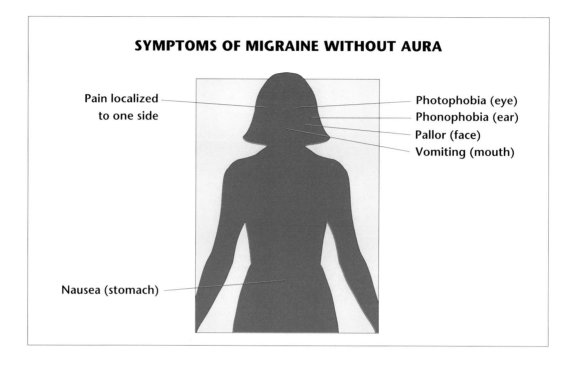

**SYMPTOMS OF MIGRAINE WITHOUT AURA**

Pain localized to one side

Photophobia (eye)
Phonophobia (ear)
Pallor (face)
Vomiting (mouth)

Nausea (stomach)

## Is it a migraine?

For quick reference here is a simple summary of symptoms that distinguish migraine from other types of headache:

- Head pain on one side, though it can sometimes affect both sides.
- Head pain which varies in severity from a dull nagging ache to unbearable pounding.
- Feeling of nausea or actual vomiting.
- Loss of appetite.
- Diarrhoea or, occasionally, constipation.
- Dislike of light and/or noise.
- Sensitivity to smells that normally may not cause offence to the sufferer.
- Pallor and cold hands and feet.
- Mood changes, depression and/or irritability.

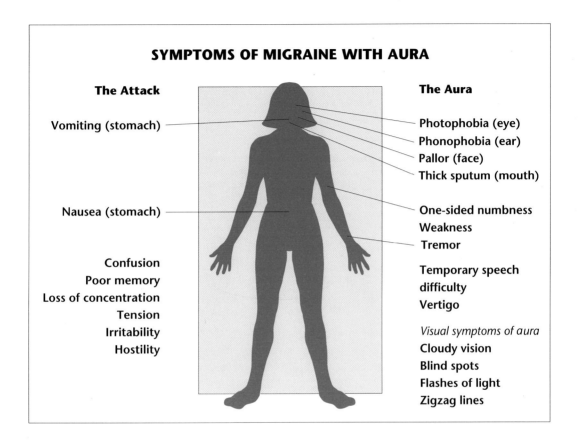

**SYMPTOMS OF MIGRAINE WITH AURA**

**The Attack**

Vomiting (stomach)

Nausea (stomach)

Confusion
Poor memory
Loss of concentration
Tension
Irritability
Hostility

**The Aura**

Photophobia (eye)
Phonophobia (ear)
Pallor (face)
Thick sputum (mouth)

One-sided numbness
Weakness
Tremor

Temporary speech
difficulty
Vertigo

*Visual symptoms of aura*
Cloudy vision
Blind spots
Flashes of light
Zigzag lines

# The stages of migraine

There are five separate stages to a migraine attack.

## Prodromal phase

The prodromal phase is the first stage in a migraine, and can affect sufferers of both classical and common migraine. It usually begins a few hours before the headache sets in, though it can start up to a day beforehand. During the prodromal phase there are often warning signs that a migraine is on its way. You may be aware of changes in your mood and behaviour, digestive disturbances, a sensation of being cold or having a stiff neck, yawning, feeling tired and irritable. Some sufferers may notice fluid retention or a craving for sweet foods.

Most people at first do not recognize that they are in the prodromal state because the symptoms are vague and indefinite, and they are often more noticeable to those around you.

# What is migraine?

Not every person who suffers migraine will go through the prodromal phase, though about one to two of every three sufferers will have some type of warning that an attack is going to occur.

## Aura phase

The second phase is the development of the aura, though not all migraine sufferers will experience it. The most common sign of this phase is visual disturbances. Your vision may be blurred, a blind

## Children and migraine

It is not only adults who suffer migraine – children are susceptible too. Migraine in children can begin at a very young age. In a group of children who had migraine at the age of seven, the average age at onset was 4.8 years.

Although before puberty boys and girls suffer about equally, as they grow older migraine becomes considerably more common in girls. And children who suffer from migraine are also more likely to experience travel sickness than those who do not develop migraine. There is evidence, too, that they often sleep badly.

There are some differences between attacks in adults and attacks in children. With children the attacks are usually much shorter, often lasting from about one to four hours – though they can last for as short a time as 30 minutes. The digestive symptoms, such as nausea, vomiting and abdominal pain, are much more common in children. In fact, when asked about their symptoms, many children barely mention the headache at all. They may also appear pale and unwell, have a fever or feel lethargic and, like adult sufferers, may dislike bright lights.

It is difficult to predict whether children who suffer migraine will grow out of it. Some studies show that a child has about a 50 per cent chance of growing into a migraine-free adult. So there is no reason to assume that if your child suffers from migraine when young, he or she will also suffer when older.

*Children as well as adults are susceptible to migraine, which can start at a very early age.*

spot may develop or you may see flashing lights. Neurological symptoms include tingling, pins and needles or difficulty in speaking.

The symptoms of an aura usually develop gradually over a period of around 20 minutes and last less than an hour. Whether visual or neurological, they gradually disappear and the headache begins to develop, usually within about an hour.

## Headache phase

The headache phase of a migraine attack can occur without your experiencing either the prodromal or the aura phase. This is the main part of the attack, and can last anywhere from four to 72 hours, which seems a horribly long time to suffer. During the headache phase,

nausea, vomiting or other digestive symptoms usually occur, as does an aversion to strong odours, such as the smell of food or cigarettes, and to bright light or noise. Many sufferers lose their appetite at this stage of the attack.

## Resolution of headache

The fourth stage is when the headache gradually becomes less severe and slowly starts to ease. This could take a few hours. You may find that you are able to sleep during this period, and in fact may wake up headache-free.

## Postdromal period

The postdromal phase occurs after the headache has gone and the attack is almost

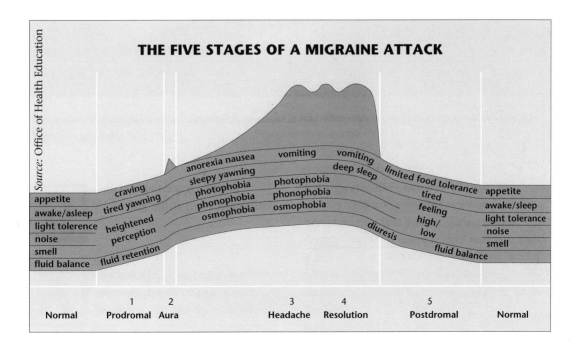

# What is migraine?

over. Many sufferers find they feel very tired, lethargic and worn out for quite some time afterwards, rather as if they have a hangover. You may notice that you have difficulty concentrating, you feel sluggish and unproductive, or do not feel very alert. You may also feel physically tired, and some sufferers find that they have aching muscles. A few sufferers feel the opposite – extremely well and full of energy.

## Who gets migraine?

Migraine is an extremely common condition. As yet there are no firm figures on exactly how many people suffer, but epidemiological (population) studies have estimated that at least five million in the UK – about 10 per cent of the population – are affected. Studies in other Western countries, such as the USA and Australia, have produced similar results.

However, this is probably a very conservative estimate. The true figures could be much higher, but because the majority of sufferers do not visit their doctor for help, it is

*Migraine attacks tend to become less frequent from around the age of 55.*

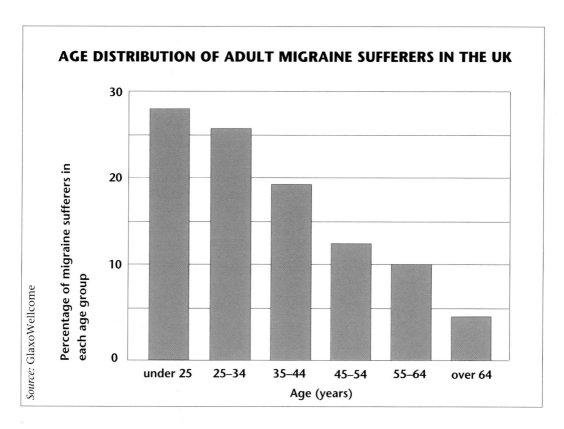

**AGE DISTRIBUTION OF ADULT MIGRAINE SUFFERERS IN THE UK**

*Percentage of migraine sufferers in each age group* — *Age (years)*

*Source: GlaxoWellcome*

difficult to be precise. Another problem with determining how many people are affected is that until 1988 there was no universally accepted definition of migraine. At that time the International Headache Society came up with a now widely accepted definition (see page 20), since when it has been much easier for doctors and scientists to identify who actually suffers from migraine and who does not.

Although it may not be known exactly how many people are affected by migraine, some factors are certain. For instance:

● At least 90 per cent of migraine sufferers have their first attack before the age of 40.

● Most sufferers experience their first migraine in their teens or twenties, although it also affects babies and young children.

● It is rare, but not unheard of, for migraine to start later in life.

● In general, attacks tend to become less frequent from around the age of 55.

● Until puberty, both boys and girls are affected equally.

● From around the time of puberty women are around three times more likely than men to suffer from migraine. Studies have indicated that about 78 per cent of migraine sufferers are female, compared with 22 per cent of men.

# What is migraine?

## The migraine personality

In the past there was a theory about a 'migraine personality'. It was thought that migraine sufferers were tense, uptight, unable to cope well with pressure and stress, and perfectionist. But a number of studies examining who experiences the condition have found no truth in this theory.

Studies have also enquired as to whether a person's race, intelligence or social class makes them more at risk of becoming a migraine sufferer. As yet no link has been shown between ethnic or social background and migraine. It seems that migraine can affect anyone – it's an 'equal opportunities' headache.

## Could it be your genes?

The argument that migraine could be an inherited condition is not a new one. Many patients are aware that at least one other member of their family suffers from migraine. But it is an extremely common condition, so if more than one person in your family is affected, it could simply be due to sheer chance rather than your genes.

*So far the existence of a 'migraine gene', making migraine an inherited condition, has not been proved.*

Experts have studied the connection between genetics and migraine. One suggestion is that people who get migraine have a different biochemical makeup from non-sufferers: they are simply more susceptible or sensitive to migraine trigger factors, rather than having been born with a special 'migraine gene'.

A gene has recently been discovered that seems to play a part in a specific type of headache – but not in migraine. As more and more genes are identified, it is possible that there may eventually turn out to be an inherited cause for migraine. However, as yet this has not been determined.

 **I often get a migraine attack first thing in the morning. When is the most common time of day for migraine to start?**

 One small US study of 15 patients found that more than half of all migraine attacks are likely to appear between six o'clock in the morning and noon. Over a 20-week period the volunteers were asked to keep diaries of their migraine attacks. When the diaries were analysed, it was found that there was a greater number of attacks between the hours of 6am and 8am, and a peak frequency between 8am and 10am. There was a noticeably lower incidence of overnight migraines – those between the hours of 8pm and 4am.

The researchers suggested that there appears to be some link between migraine and our body's circadian rhythms – our body clock – which is also seen in other medical conditions: for instance, heart attack. Further research to study the circadian rhythm of migraine could help to improve our understanding and possibly lead to more effective treatments.

*Chapter two*

# Different types of migraine

There are two main types of migraine: common migraine, known as migraine without aura, and classical migraine, now medically called migraine with aura. There is no fundamental difference between the two, and the mechanism that causes the attack appears to be the same for both. The difference lies in whether the sufferer develops an aura beforehand.

**Common migraine** is, just as the name suggests, the most common type, accounting for about 65 per cent of attacks. Like classical migraine it usually starts with the prodromal or first stage, but there is no aura. The migraine headache then develops gradually while, at the same time, building in intensity. The headache is usually accompanied by nausea or vomiting, or a dislike of noise or light. A number of hours later the headache gradually disappears and the

sufferer will then pass into the resolution and postdromal phases of the attack.

**Classical migraine** (with aura) is the more dramatic of the two types, but less common. About 35 per cent of sufferers experience this kind of migraine.

It is possible for an individual to suffer from both varieties of migraine. About 70 per cent of people who have migraine with aura also experience attacks without aura. Interestingly about 1 per cent of sufferers have simply the aura alone – they do not go on to develop the headache or other symptoms commonly associated with a migraine attack.

The pain of the headache is said to be equally intense with or without an aura. And the treatment is the same for both types of migraine, including conventional drug therapy or self-help remedies.

## Defining migraine

In the past it was difficult for doctors to agree on a definition of what constitutes migraine. In 1988, however, the International Headache Society, a group of doctors and experts concerned with the study, research and treatment of headache and migraine, came

together and agreed on a definition of migraine.

This is now fairly widely accepted throughout the medical profession and is a useful diagnostic tool for doctors. Their conclusions on the two main types of migraine are outlined on page 21.


**20**

## **Without aura (common migraine)***

An individual is classified as suffering from migraine without aura if they have had at least five attacks which meet the following criteria:

● headache lasting from four to 72 hours (untreated or unsuccessfully treated);
● headache with at least two of the following characteristics:
– unilateral location;
– pulsating quality;
– moderate to severe intensity;
– aggravated by movement;
● during headache, at least one of the following associated symptoms:
– nausea and/or vomiting;
– photophobia and/or phonophobia.

## **With aura (classical migraine)***

An individual is classified as suffering from migraine with aura if, in addition to the migraine symptoms defined above, they have had at least two attacks which include at least three of the following characteristics:
● one or more fully reversible aura symptoms (for example, flashing lights, unilateral numbness);
● at least one aura symptom developing gradually over more than four minutes,

*The pain of a migraine headache is said to be equally intense with or without aura.*

or two or more symptoms occurring in succession;
● no aura symptom lasting more than 60 minutes (if more than one aura symptom is present, the accepted duration is proportionally increased);
● headache pain experienced within 60 minutes of the aura, although it may begin before.

* *International Headache Society, 'Classification and Diagnostic Criteria for Headache Disorders, Cranial Neuralgias and Facial Pain', Cephalalgia 1988, 8 (Supplement 7), pages 19–28.*

# Different types of migraine

## Other varieties of migraine

● **Opthalmoplegic migraine** is uncommon and usually occurs in children up to around the age of ten or 12. There is often a family history of migraine, though not necessarily this type. In addition to the headache, which is often centred around the eye, there can be weakness of the muscles surrounding the eye, leading to a droopy eyelid, along with dilated pupils and double vision or other eyesight problems.

● **Basilar artery migraine,** another rare form, causes headache, usually over the back of the head, along with dizziness, unsteadiness or difficulty in talking. The symptoms are thought to be due to a disturbance of the blood supply to a major brain artery. Pre-headache symptoms include vertigo (a feeling that the world is spinning around), double vision and poor muscular co-ordination.

● **Hemiplegic migraine,** which is very rare, causes a temporary paralysis or weakness on one side of the body, usually on the same side in each attack, and the headache can last for a week or longer. In many instances there is a family history of similar attacks. Some people may experience vision problems and vertigo in the time before the onset of the headache.

● **Status migrainosus** is a rare and severe type of migraine that can last 72 hours or longer. The pain and nausea are so intense that people who have this type of headache are usually hospitalized for treatment. The use of certain drugs can trigger status migrainosus.

● **Headache-free migraine** is characterized by the aura alone, not followed by a headache. More rarely common migraine symptoms such as visual problems, nausea, vomiting or diarrhoea may occur without a headache. Some headache specialists have suggested that unexplained pain in a particular part of the body, fever and dizziness could also be types of headache-free migraine.

The treatment for all these types of migraine is the same as for classical or common migraine. Before a diagnosis is made, however, all other possible diagnoses must be excluded. It is likely that your doctor may refer you to a specialist such as a neurologist for investigations and testing, such as brain scans.

**A friend of mine said that she gets the migraine aura but doesn't go on to develop the headache. Is this possible?**

Yes, it is. It's been recognized that some people who suffer from classical migraine (that is, migraine with aura) do occasionally experience the aura alone. They may suffer the other symptoms, such as nausea and vomiting, but not the headache. This often occurs as the sufferer gets older, and some people do find that the headaches disappear completely, although the auras continue.

**How do I know if I'm getting a migraine?**

Many – but not all – sufferers go through the prodromal phase. This is when the warning signs of an impending attack will appear. The signs and symptoms can be very slight or subtle, and it is not always easy to recognize them. You may find that you have a change in mood, becoming either very depressed or almost 'manic'. You may yawn a lot, seem clumsy, or feel tired or irritable.

The best advice is to try to become familiar with your symptoms during the prodromal phase. And ask your family to help you, as they are often better at spotting the changes than you yourself are. The sooner you realize an attack is on the way, the sooner you can begin to take action – for instance, by taking any medication or making sure that you get enough rest.

One problem with the prodromal phase is that it can make it difficult to separate out possible migraine triggers from prodromal activity. Some sufferers find that during this phase they crave sugary foods such as chocolate. As a result they then blame these foods for causing the attack when in fact the migraine has already started. Becoming familiar with your prodromal symptoms, therefore, can also help you to learn more about the correct triggers for your migraine and eventually enable you to manage attacks more effectively.

*Chapter three*

# The mystery
# of migraine

In spite of all the continuing studies which are attempting to unravel the mystery of migraine, scientists and doctors are still not yet clear about its precise cause. Most accept that it occurs as a result of changes in blood flow within the brain, but they differ on why this develops in the first place.

There are two main schools of thought. Some specialists believe that the development of migraine stems from vascular changes: that is, the way in which the blood vessels in the skull and brain are functioning. The adherents to the vascular school of thought are of the opinion that, for some unknown reason, certain blood vessels in the brain shut down.

However, many others are convinced that it could be a neurological problem, or a problem in the way in which the brain itself is working. They believe that there is some type of change in the way the brain controls the blood vessels, opening them as well as closing them down; and that during a migraine the blood vessels respond to unknown changes that occur within the brain tissue.

Regardless of whether the initial abnormality is a vascular or neurological problem, it has long been thought that the initial symptoms of migraine are probably due to a sudden constriction in some of the blood vessels in the brain. The headache comes on as these constricted vessels dilate, or widen, and blood surges through the sensitive tissue. And the final result of all this closing and opening of blood vessels is a migraine attack. However, new research indicates that the real mechanism is not as straightforward as this scenario suggests, and until more research is done the actual events remain a mystery.

## Changes in blood flow

A great deal of research is taking place to try to gain a better understanding why there should be changes in the blood flow and blood vessels in the brain of migraine sufferers. Many experts and scientists are of the view that people who get migraine headaches have blood vessels that are oversensitive – that is, they overreact – to various trigger factors. So they have developed a theory about migraine that explains these blood-flow changes.

According to this theory, your nervous system responds to a trigger, such as stress, certain foods, your environment, or an alteration in your usual sleeping pattern, by creating a spasm in the nerve-rich arteries at the base of the brain. The spasm constricts, or closes down, several arteries supplying blood to the brain, including the scalp artery and the carotid or neck arteries. As these arteries constrict, the flow of blood to the brain is reduced in certain vessels.

At the same time, tiny cells called platelets (which circulate in the bloodstream and are responsible for helping blood to clot) clump together. During this process the platelets release a chemical called serotonin. Serotonin is a powerful constrictor of arteries. It also acts as a neurotransmitter – a chemical that sends messages back and forth between your brain cells (see the box below).

## The role of serotonin

Much research is taking place into the role of serotonin, also known as 5-HT (5 hydroxytryptamine), in the development of migraine attacks. This chemical, called a neurotransmitter, occurs naturally in plants and animals. In humans it is found in many parts of the body, especially in the blood platelets and in the gut. A small amount is found in the brain.

Serotonin has many effects in the body with regard to migraine. For example, the nausea and vomiting that are common symptoms of migraine are thought to be triggered by a release of serotonin within the vomiting centre of the brain. Another theory is that they could result from an increase in sensations received from the vagus nerve which runs from the brain to the stomach, again as a result of serotonin being released in the stomach and intestines.

When serotonin is released from its storage sites during migraine, it tends to constrict some blood vessels and dilate others, which can lead to the pain of a migraine headache.

As a result of these discoveries about the role of serotonin, new migraine medications have been developed that can block some of the effects. As scientists understand more about how serotonin affects the blood vessels in the brain, they may well be able to understand more about migraine too.

# The mystery of migraine

Source: Glaxo Wellcome

## HOW SEROTONIN (5-HT) MAY AFFECT BLOOD VESSELS

**Pre-migraine phase**
5-HT released from blood platelets

**Aura phase**
Temporary constriction of large cerebral arteries

**Headache**
Low 5-HT levels causing painful widening of the cranial blood vessels

*Serotonin appears to affect both the dilation (widening) and constriction (narrowing) of blood vessels. This, in turn, can lead to aura and the headache of migraine.*

## Why does it hurt?

Many people with migraine or headache wrongly assume that it is their brain or skull that is the source of their agony. However, the bones of the skull and tissues of the brain itself never hurt, because they lack pain-sensitive nerve fibres. Instead it is the swelling of the blood vessels, which in turn stretch the nerve fibres, that causes the pain.

There are several areas of nerves in the head that can hurt. These include a network of nerves that extends over the scalp, and also certain nerves in the face, mouth and throat. The muscles of the head and the blood vessels along the surface and at the base of the brain can also hurt because they too contain the delicate nerve fibres that are sensitive to pain.

The ends of all these pain-sensitive nerves, called nociceptors, can be stimulated by any number of triggers that cause migraine, including stress, muscular tension and certain foods and drinks. Once the nociceptors have been stimulated by a trigger, they send a message up the length of the nerve fibre to the nerve cells in the brain. The message relayed is that a part of the body hurts. And the message is determined by the location of the nociceptor. For example, a person who realizes that his or her hand hurts is responding to nociceptors in the hand, while a headache is due to stimulated nociceptors in the head.

## Chapter four

# What triggers a migraine?

Although headache and migraine experts do not know exactly why people develop migraine, it is known that certain factors are often involved in triggering an attack. These trigger factors seem to act on the hypothalamus in the brain. This part of the brain is responsible for controlling a number of physiological functions, including body temperature, appetite, your mood and emotions, your reaction to stress and even menstruation. And the hypothalamus is a prime storage area of the neurotransmitter serotonin (see page 25). So it may be that when your body comes into contact with enough of these triggers, it causes the release of serotonin from the hypothalamus, which in turn kicks off a migraine.

There is a number of common well-known triggers for migraine, though not every trigger will affect every sufferer. The specific triggers can vary from sufferer to sufferer, and even from attack to attack. For example, you may find that drinking red wine during a late night

usually leads to a migraine within the next few days. Occasionally, however, you find that you can have a glass of wine with no ill effects. And if you have suffered from migraine for a long time, you may notice that the specific triggers for an attack have changed over this period.

It is also important to note that, in general, it is rare for contact with one trigger alone to lead to a migraine. It is much more common that you need two or three in combination before an attack is brought on. And it may also depend on the amount of the trigger you have encountered. As mentioned, one glass of red wine might not cause any problems, but two or three glasses could. This is often known as a trigger threshold, and each individual sufferer will have a level below which triggers are unlikely to cause an attack. However, once you reach or exceed that threshold, it is more likely that an attack will occur. This is one reason why keeping a record of your possible triggers, or trying to determine which affect you, can help you discover your personal threshold.

## The common triggers

If you are one of those born with a susceptibility to migraine, you are going to be

more vulnerable to a headache caused by substances or factors that are not harmful or

# What triggers a migraine?

dangerous to others. It is not unlike the problems hay fever sufferers experience. For many of us pollen does not lead to any allergic reaction, but in people susceptible to hay fever it causes the sneezing, runny eyes and itchy nose so common in the summer months.

A similar state of affairs exists regarding migraine. It may be hard to believe that seemingly harmless foods such as nuts or oranges, or a change in the weather, can result in a painful migraine headache. Yet if you are one of the millions born with the potential to get migraine, it is certainly true.

## Dietary factors

Food is thought to be a common trigger factor. Studies have indicated that around 20 per cent of migraine sufferers can link certain foods to the onset of an attack. Common ones include chocolate, cheese, red wine and citrus fruits. It is not known why foods will set off a migraine: some experts believe it could be a type of allergic reaction, others are looking at specific chemicals or ingredients in the foods that might affect the blood vessels. One likely explanation is that during the prodromal phase the sufferer craves certain foods and incorrectly

*Cheese and red wine – a tempting sight, but they could trigger a migraine attack in some people.*

blames these foods for causing the headache.

Whatever the mechanism, many people believe that certain foods will cause a migraine even if there is no evidence for this. They then strictly avoid these foods without first finding out if they really contribute to their own migraine.

The best way for you to discover whether foods affect you adversely is to discuss with your doctor about keeping a trigger diary. This is a record of any common triggers you have come into contact with in the hours before the migraine: if foods are a trigger, they will usually bring on a migraine within one or two hours of being eaten.

Once you have pinpointed certain suspect foods, you can then work out a plan to omit them from your diet, often called an elimination diet. But this must be done correctly and carefully. Pick one food at a time and omit it for about a month. Keep a note to determine if the attacks improve: for instance, if they are less frequent or less severe. If they are, you slowly reintroduce the food and see if the migraines return to their former level. If they do, it is likely that the food in question is a trigger. If they do not, you try the same procedure with another foodstuff.

It is important that you do this one step at a time. If you eliminate too many foods at once, you will have no way of knowing which ones might be contributing to your migraine.

Probably the most common dietary trigger is not a specific food but a lack of or insufficient food. Many people find that if they miss a meal or go without food for too long, a migraine results. It is suspected that this is a result of the drop in blood sugar levels that accompanies lack of food and hunger.

The best advice for people with migraine is to make sure that you develop a routine to your meals. Try to eat at about the same time each day, making sure that you do not go too long between meals. Have a good breakfast, avoid fasting and dieting and try to avoid eating 'on the run'. It may be that you need to have a small snack mid-morning and mid-afternoon to avoid a migraine. Although this may be inconvenient, it is certainly much better than falling ill later with a full-blown attack.

## Sleeping patterns

The relationship between sleep and migraine is a strange one. While it is true that napping or sleeping during an acute attack can often hasten your recovery, getting too much or too little sleep can trigger a migraine. Many people find that they suffer an attack when their sleeping patterns are unsettled. This could be due to working on a big project, when they are staying up late and getting up early. Or it could be at the weekend or on holiday, when they take advantage of the extra time and have a good lie-in.

To see if sleep has an effect on your migraines, you can experiment with your sleeping patterns just as you can with food. First try to establish regular sleeping patterns. This means going to bed and getting up at around the same time, including on the weekends. Some sufferers are so sensitive to sleep changes that even an hour more or less can make a huge difference and bring on a raging attack.

# What triggers a migraine?

Once your sleeping patterns have been established, you can then begin to sleep in for an hour or so and see if this makes any difference to the type and frequency of your migraines. Try to do this over a period of, say, a couple of weeks, as it may be that sleeping in needs to be combined with another trigger to bring on a migraine. Then you can try staying up later a few nights to see what effect this has. If you remain migraine-free, or if your migraines follow their usual pattern, it could be that a change in sleeping habits is not one of your triggers.

## Environmental factors

There are so many aspects of our environment that could be possible trigger factors. The list is almost endless, but the common ones include noise, light, heat, smoke and strong smells. Even changes in the weather can affect those sufferers who are vulnerable.

Unfortunately few of us have complete control over our environment. In some cases simply avoiding smoky or stuffy rooms, opening windows to let in fresh air and trying to keep noise pollution to minimum can help. However, if you are aware that a migraine is

*Environmental factors can trigger a migraine in some sufferers. No doubt the smog hanging over London on this hot sunny day was responsible for more than a few.*

likely to occur if you cannot avoid environmental triggers, this makes it easier to be prepared for an attack. You can then take any medication at the first warning signs, and hopefully reduce its severity or possibly even stop it completely.

## Physical exercise

Although regular exercise can help reduce your stress levels, which is certainly useful for migraine sufferers, in some people the exercise itself can bring on an attack. In most cases it is not every-day moderate exercise that causes migraine but rather overdoing it or exercising suddenly if you have not done so in a while.

Regular exercise is a crucial part of healthy living for everyone, so do not consider giving it up. Instead make sure that you do not exercise excessively.

You may find that taking glucose tablets while exercising or making sure that you have had a light carbohydrate-rich snack beforehand can help to keep your blood sugar levels steady during your workout. And this may help to prevent an attack from starting.

## Checklist of common triggers

Many triggers for migraine are the same ones that can trigger a different type of headache – for instance, a tension headache. By using this checklist of common triggers, you can try to trace or detect what you might be susceptible to. Then, whenever possible, you can either avoid the trigger altogether or be prepared that a migraine might occur if you do encounter the trigger.

● **Lack of food** Missing or delaying meals, fasting or dieting, eating too little or too much, skipping breakfast.

● **Specific foods** Chocolate, red wine, cheese, citrus fruits, coffee, tea, alcohol, nuts, meats, dairy products.

● **Smoking** Being in a smoky environment or smoking yourself.

● **Sleep** Getting too much or too little sleep, having irregular sleeping patterns, disturbed sleep.

● **Hormonal changes** Before or during menstruation, pregnancy, taking the oral contraceptive pill, menopause and hormone replacement therapy.

● **Environmental factors** Heat, cold, light, noise, changes in the weather, flickering lights, cinemas, strong odours, parties, travelling.

● **Physical activity** During or after exercise, during or after sex, lifting or straining, shopping.

● **Stress** Anxiety, depression, being under pressure at home or at work, school worries, money worries.

# What triggers a migraine?

**Which foods are more likely to trigger a migraine?**

A number of specific foods have been blamed for causing migraine attacks. The three Cs – chocolate, cheese and citrus fruits – are the ones most commonly mentioned by sufferers. It's not exactly certain why this should be.

Some studies have pinpointed chemicals in fatty foods, called vasodilating amines, that widen the blood vessels. The amines are absorbed more easily when fat is present. This could be why fatty foods such as chocolate and cheese top the list.

Another widely blamed culprit is red wine. It's thought that chemicals called flavenoids (which give red wine its colour) inhibit the effectiveness of a special enzyme that works to detoxify, or make harmless, a particular group of chemicals in the intestine. And when we develop an overload of these chemicals, they can lead to migraine and headache symptoms.

However, there is any number of foods that have been said to cause migraine. Some sufferers find that they have an attack after eating Chinese food or hot dogs. In these instances it is suspected that a food additive, monosodium glutamate, which is used as a flavour enhancer, is the migraine trigger. And nitrites, which are used in the curing of meats such as ham and salami, also work as vasodilators, widening the blood vessels. Avoiding these foods could therefore help ease your attacks.

Surprisingly ice cream has also been known to bring on a migraine. In this case the sudden shock of eating something very cold, rather than any one chemical or ingredient in the ice cream itself, is thought to be the cause.

**Do food allergies lead to migraine?**

This theory has been around for quite some time. Although there is a great deal of anecdotal evidence about the role that 'food allergy' plays in migraine, it is not supported by laboratory or scientific studies. Currently it is believed that migraine due to food allergy is a rare occurrence.

Part of the difficulty is that there are no effective tests for true food allergy. Although certain foods do play a part in triggering an attack, it is usually caused by chemicals or ingredients in these foods rather than a true allergic response. In fact the term 'food intolerance' is now more generally accepted than 'food allergy'.

If you suspect that a food is contributing to your migraines, the best way to discover if it actually has an effect is to eliminate it from your diet. Do this for a couple of months, keeping an attack diary (see page 39) at the same time. If you notice a change in your migraine patterns, it could be that specific food plays a part. If there is no change, you can re-introduce the food and go on to try another.

*Citrus fruit may look delicious, but many migraine sufferers have to avoid eating it as they believe that it triggers attacks.*

**Can sexual intercourse cause a migraine?**

Sex, as with exercise, can bring on a headache and occasionally a full-blown migraine attack. It usually occurs at or near the time of orgasm and can be very severe. However, in most cases the pain usually lasts only a few minutes, but it can continue after intercourse for up to a day or so. And women, as well as men, can suffer headaches during sex.

It's not known exactly why this occurs. One suggestion is that it is due to physiological changes that take place during sex. Your blood pressure can rise dramatically and your pulse rate almost double. Another theory is that it is caused by muscular tension in the shoulders and neck, but as yet experts are just not sure. If you suffer from headaches or migraine that seem to be linked with making love, do see your doctor.

# What triggers a migraine?

## Stress

A number of sufferers find a definite link between stress and their migraines. Interestingly the migraines rarely occur exactly when you are anxious and under pressure, but they tend to come on after the stressful period in your life, when you are trying to get back to normal. This could be why some sufferers get weekend migraines – they are winding down after the pressures of the workplace, and in doing so trigger an attack.

The best way of handling stress is to find ways to cope with it more effectively: for example, you could try learning a relaxation technique. You should also take a careful look at your lifestyle to see if there are practical ways in which to reduce your stress load (see Chapter 5).

## *Migraine in women*

Women are most susceptible to headaches in general, and studies have shown that they are three times more prone to suffer migraine than men. This vulnerability may be due to fluctuating hormone levels throughout the month and, indeed, throughout their lifespan. Although in children about equal numbers of boys and girls suffer, as they hit the teenage years the number of girls far outweighs the boys. It is thought that these differences which begin to appear at puberty may be down to the effects of female hormones.

The most common times for women to notice changes in their migraine attacks is

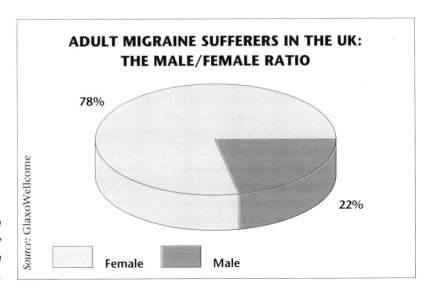

**ADULT MIGRAINE SUFFERERS IN THE UK: THE MALE/FEMALE RATIO**

78%

22%

*Source:* GlaxoWellcome

Female    Male

*Slightly more than three times as many women as men suffer from migraine.*

during menstruation, when they are pregnant and around the time of the menopause. They may also notice that their migraines change if they start the oral contraceptive pill.

## Menstrual migraine

Since the time of Hippocrates, when a link between migraine and menstruation was first noted, it was thought that the uterus, or womb, was the original source of the symptoms and pain. It is now known that the hypothalamus, the region in the brain that appears to react to migraine triggers, also controls the menstrual cycle. And in some way this may be why women suffer migraine around the time of their periods.

Menstrual migraine is common, and one study at the City of London Migraine Clinic found that around 50 per cent of women questioned felt their migraines were linked to their periods. Of these, 15 per cent said that they had their first migraine attack in the same year as they had their first period.

Menstrual migraine is usually defined as a migraine that occurs within two days of the period starting, and in the first three days of bleeding. But it is not accompanied by migraines at any other times of the month. It is thought that this pattern coincides with the phase of the menstrual cycle when the hormones oestrogen and progesterone are at their lowest. Many other women can link their migraines to menstruation, but have attacks at other times of the month as well: this is called menstrually related migraine.

Separating these two groups is important. Women with menstrual migraine appear to be affected by the drop in oestrogen that naturally occurs during the menstrual cycle. These women may simply be more sensitive to normal hormonal fluctuations. Women with menstrually related migraine seem to be affected by hormonal changes, but are obviously susceptible to other migraine triggers too.

Although it may appear that hormones are the only important factor in menstrual migraines, if this were the case, oestrogen supplements would always help every women. But studies have shown that they do not. Research is taking place to try to determine the role played by other chemicals and hormones besides oestrogen, which also change with the menstrual cycle.

## The effect of the pill

The combined oral contraceptive pill contains both oestrogen and progesterone, the two hormones thought to play a part in migraine. But the effects that the pill has on different migraine sufferers will vary from woman to woman. Some who start the pill find their attacks become more frequent and severe, often with attacks occurring in the pill-free week, while others find their situation improves dramatically. However, the majority of women who take the pill do not notice much of a change in their migraine pattern.

Most doctors feel that is is safe for women who suffer common migraine to take the combined contraceptive pill. Women who experience migraine with aura, the so-called classical migraine, though, should consider a different form of contraception. The same is

# What triggers a migraine?

true for women who have migraine without aura, but who begin to experience migraine with aura when they start the pill. It is safe for these women to take the progestogen-only or mini-pill, which does not contain any oestrogen.

 **I get the occasional migraine and wonder if it is safe to take the contraceptive pill?**

 Women who suffer from migraine with aura (classical migraine) should not use the combined oral contraceptive pill. However, the progestogen-only or mini-pill is safe to use. If you have migraine without aura, you can take the combined pill, but you may find that you experience migraine attacks during the pill-free week, when your oestrogen level falls. And if you find that the pattern of your migraine alters when you start the combined pill, you should always discuss this with your doctor to see if it is safe to continue or if you should consider an alternative form of contraception.

## Pregnancy and migraine

It is estimated that around 70–75 per cent of women who regularly suffer migraines find the only time they are migraine-free, or that their migraines ease up and become much less frequent or severe, is during pregnancy. But this is not true for every woman. In some instances headaches can become considerably worse, especially in the early weeks of pregnancy. And, rarely, women may have their first migraine

during pregnancy, or notice that the type of migraine changes and they begin to have auras along with their other symptoms.

There is a number of explanations for these changes. The improvement could be due to the anti-inflammatory effects of certain female hormones that are racing around the body during pregnancy. Another possible explanation could be the effect of endorphins, the body's natural painkillers. The level of endorphins is often much higher during pregnancy, but declines rapidly after delivery and the headaches return. Another explanation is the gradual increase in oestrogen levels.

Treating migraine in pregnancy can be difficult because pregnant women should avoid taking any medication that may cross the placenta and affect the developing baby. Before taking any medication, including over-the-counter painkillers, discuss it with your doctor or midwife first, although paracetamol is known to be safe.

If you are affected by migraine while pregnant, make special efforts to take care of yourself. Eat small frequent meals throughout the day. This helps to avoid a drop in blood sugar levels that may trigger an attack. Be sure to get enough rest, and try to reduce your stress levels. Try to keep to your normal routine as closely as possible. This will help to ensure that your migraine triggers are kept to a minimum.

## Menopause and migraine

Menopause is the time when the ovaries start producing smaller quantities of oestrogen, the female hormone. During the menopause it is not unusual for women to find that their

*The majority of female migraine sufferers find that their attacks become less severe or cease altogether during pregnancy.*

# What triggers a migraine?

migraine attacks become more frequent or severe. Studies investigating the effect of menopause on migraine have shown that in about 45 per cent of women the attacks are made worse, between 30 and 45 per cent do not notice any change, and about 15 per cent notice an improvement.

Fortunately, after the menopause, the majority of women find that their migraines settle and grow less frequent and severe. In fact migraine in general tends to become less frequent after around the age of 55 – this is true for male as well as female sufferers.

## Migraine and HRT

Hormone replacement therapy (HRT) is a way of replacing the oestrogen that is produced in lower quantities during and after the menopause. It is also used to help alleviate many of the symptoms of menopause, such as depression, hot flushes, night sweats and mood changes. It also, of course, helps prevent osteoporosis (weakening of the bones) and appears to protect against heart disease.

As yet it is impossible to tell exactly what effects HRT has on migraine. As with the contraceptive pill or pregnancy, some women find that their migraines improve with HRT, but others find that it aggravates their condition.

The only certain way to know how it will affect you is to try it. There is a wide variety of methods to choose from, including pills, patches, injections and implants. You must give it a chance to work, so it is recommended that you take HRT for at least six months. After this time you will be able to tell whether it has had any effect on your migraines. If one formulation does not provide the benefits you want, talk to your doctor about changing to another or to a different way of taking it. It is to be hoped that you will find one that improves your migraines without causing too many side effects which are difficult for you to cope with.

## Chapter five

# Managing your migraine

In spite of the fact that there is help available for migraine – although there is no cure – the majority of sufferers, about 70 per cent, manage their migraine on their own without seeing a doctor. However, this does not mean that migraine does not affect their life in any way.

Many sufferers are able to continue to work and care for their homes and families fairly normally during an attack. Some try to struggle on throughout the day in the fear that others will not take their migraine seriously, yet many find that they can do little more than lie down in a quiet dark place and wait for the attack to run its course.

Fortunately the majority of sufferers have infrequent attacks and do manage to cope, primarily with the help of over-the-counter painkillers and headache remedies. Usually only if the attacks become more frequent or severe do they seek help from their doctor. It is a pity to wait until this stage, because your doctor can help you find ways of coping with migraine more effectively (see Chapter 6). You are more likely to be successful in managing your migraines if you can enlist the help of your doctor or a specialist migraine clinic, and the support and sympathy of your family and friends.

Regardless of whether you have decided to cope on your own or have already been to the doctor for advice, there is a number of ways to help you live with your condition. Finding out what works for you is crucial – it will not be the same for every sufferer, just as the migraine attacks themselves can vary from person to person.

## Preventing an attack

Although there are no guaranteed methods of preventing an attack, becoming familiar with the pattern of lifestyle and triggers that may lead to your experiencing a migraine provides you with ammunition possibly to ward it off or at least to keep it under control.

### Keeping an attack diary

The first step is to keep an accurate record, or diary, of your attacks. This helps both you and your doctor to recognize any pattern that may develop. While in the throws of an attack, you may swear faithfully that you will keep a diary. But when the attack subsides, you forget about

# Managing your migraine

*Keeping a diary of your migraine attacks and potential triggers will arm you with information to help control the attacks.*

the pain and discomfort – until the next time. The best solution is to keep a notepad or notebook by your bedside or somewhere handy around the house. Every time you suffer an attack make a note of:
- the date of the attack;
- the day of the week;
- the time when the attack started;
- what symptoms you have;
- if the symptoms changed during the attack and in what way;
- how long the attack lasted;

- what treatment you took, if any;
- what time you took the treatment;
- how effective it was;
- when the attack ended;
- how you felt when the attack was over.

You should do this for at least five or six attacks in a row. You will then have enough information about your migraines to analyse. Taking a good look at this information could help to show you and your doctor if there is any pattern to your attacks. It can also help indicate what treatments are more effective, and whether or not your migraines are changing in any way.

## Keeping a trigger diary

It is also a good idea to try to keep a trigger diary, though you may need some advice from your doctor on the best way to do this. Trigger diaries can help you to determine what specific factors might contribute to setting off your migraine attacks.

It is likely that you will already be aware of at least a few of your migraine triggers. However, it is unlikely that every time you encounter one of these factors you will get a migraine, which can be very confusing. It is common for most sufferers to need more than one trigger before a migraine develops. This is why keeping a record or diary of potential triggers can help you determine which are most relevant for you and also what your trigger threshold is, or how many triggers you need before a migraine starts.

Buy a notebook and try to keep it with you at all times. Every day or evening jot down the potential triggers you have encountered. You might find it easier to make a list of common triggers and photocopy the list. Then each night just tick off the ones you have encountered, such as shopping, stress at work or having a drink at lunchtime. This is important, as when a migraine does occur you are unlikely to be able to remember what you have done in the days or hours immediately prior to the attack.

Women should also keep a record of their menstrual cycle or any symptoms of premenstrual syndrome (PMS) they have noticed. And do not forget to write down any medication you take regularly, including natural remedies, vitamin and mineral supplements or the contraceptive pill.

## Interpreting the diaries

After you have had about five or six migraine attacks, you should have enough information in both your attack and trigger diaries to start drawing some conclusions. Compare the timing of your attacks with the triggers you have come into contact with. Note if there was a build-up of triggers, if you simply had a few bad days that led to an attack, or if you had any warning signs that should have given you a clue that a migraine was on its way.

Once you have done this, try to determine which triggers you can do something about, such as missing meals or sitting in smoky pubs, and those you cannot control, such as your menstrual cycle or shopping. Then work out a plan to deal with the triggers over which you have some influence. For example, this may mean sitting down to meals at regular times, ensuring that you get enough sleep, or avoiding

certain foods that lead to trouble.

If you are uncertain about which triggers or combination of triggers seem to be the possible culprits, try to avoid them one at a time – rather as if you were following an exclusion diet. Do this for about a month and see if it makes a difference. This is not always easy, as determining which triggers or combination of factors are important in your case can sometimes be difficult. For this reason it is a good idea to work out a plan of action with your family doctor. Then the two of you can chart your progress together and have a better chance of finding answers to what causes your migraines.

Of course, it is not worth identifying your trigger factors if you are not willing to make a commitment to changing your lifestyle to avoid – or incorporate – some healthier habits. There is no point in realizing that red wine gives you a migraine unless you are either willing to forego it or live with the consequences.

However, knowing which triggers may lead to a migraine can help you be more prepared for an attack. Of course there are some triggers you can do little about, but in these cases at least you will have the knowledge that a migraine may occur within a certain period of time, and you can be alert to the warning symptoms, such as tiredness and yawning, changes in mood or behaviour or being extra-sensitive to noise and light. This helps you be prepared, so you can treat a migraine in the very early stages. And although it may not ward off the migraine altogether, it may lessen the headache and discomfort.

# Managing your migraine

## What to do during an attack

In addition to taking your medication (see the box on page 43), follow the advice given below. Although nausea and vomiting are common symptoms of migraine, it is a good idea to try to eat something during an attack. You may find that eating plain bland foods such as dry toast or biscuits can help ease any nausea you are experiencing. And of course if you do vomit it is less painful to have something to throw up than vomiting on an empty stomach. However, many sufferers find that they lose their appetite during an attack. If the thought or smell of food makes you feel worse, do not force yourself to try to eat something.

Some sufferers find they crave carbohydrate foods or chocolate during a migraine, while others like sugary fizzy drinks. You may need to follow your instincts until you find the combination that works for you.

Ideally you should lie down in a quiet dark room and let the attack take its course. Ask friends and family to keep the noise level down, close the blinds or curtains and put on a sleep mask if you need to.

*During a migraine attack some sufferers crave chocolate or other carbohydrates.*

## Taking the tablets

One of the key factors in coping with migraine is ensuring that you take any medication early enough in the attack. This can make all the difference to the severity of the attack, and in some instances ward it off altogether.

● Take any migraine medication at the first sign of an attack. If you take it when the attack is in full swing, it will have little effect. Part of the reason for this is that the stomach is considerably less active during a migraine – it goes into a condition known as 'stasis' – so any drug you take by mouth will not be digested and absorbed as it would normally.

● Take your migraine tablets with water or a drink to help them go down more easily.

● If possible, take your tablets on an empty stomach. They will be absorbed and begin working far more quickly than when you have a full stomach. And if you have eaten a fatty meal beforehand this will inhibit absorption even more.

● Always stick to the prescribed dosage.

You might find that putting a hot water bottle or even an ice pack on the part of your head that hurts the most can help. And a number of studies have found that sleep can work wonders for a migraine and helps to speed recovery. But not every sufferer finds this convenient or feasible.

If you cannot stop what you are doing, do try to take on less detailed work while you are having a migraine, because your concentration will not be at its best. And put off any projects or chores that are not absolutely necessary until the attack has passed and you are feeling better able to cope.

## A migraine-free lifestyle

As well as learning to manage your migraine attacks, it is important that you make an effort to make some changes in your lifestyle if you suspect they are contributing to your condition. Some of the changes are ones from which all of us could benefit, even if they do not have a direct effect on your migraine.

Others are specific to migraine and should be able to make a real difference.

### Look at your diet

Once you have interpreted your trigger diary, you may have some ideas about what foods may lead to have a migraine attack. You might

# Managing your migraine

also have a pretty good idea of whether your eating habits could use some adjusting.

If there are specific foods that you are certain cause you to have a migraine, the only practical advice is to avoid them if possible. You may also be able to eat small amounts of these foods without their causing problems, but to determine this will be a matter of trial and error.

Equally important is to make sure that you eat regularly throughout the day to avoid sudden drops in your blood sugar level. Breakfast is an important meal for migraine sufferers, even if it is simply toast and juice.

*It is especially important for migraine sufferers never to skip breakfast – the aim is to maintain a steady blood sugar level.*

Avoid missing meals or rushing through a meal – all can have negative effects on your ability to avoid a migraine. You may also find it easier to eat small meals frequently throughout the day. Again this will keep your blood sugar level steady. And avoid strict dieting or fasting, as this also has the effect of lowering the blood sugar level.

## Reduce your stress levels

The amount of stress you are under can have a number of profound effects on your ability to avoid a migraine. One reason is that when you are under a lot of stress, you tend to let any healthy routines fall by the wayside. This may lead to less control over triggers – you may be missing meals, having sleepless nights and foregoing exercise. Another is that when we are in stressful situations our bodies release chemicals and hormones into the bloodstream that may play a part in the migraine process. Interestingly people who suffer migraines due to stress tend to get them after the stressful period has passed rather than during it. For example, it is common to have a migraine at the weekend after a hectic week at work, or on holiday when you are trying to wind down.

Learning to reduce the amount of stress in your life can make a real difference, and can also give you more control over trigger factors. Stress reduction can help you get into a routine and have a more structured lifestyle.

There are any number of stress-reduction techniques you can use, including breathing exercises, relaxation exercises, yoga, meditation and even physical exercise. There are plenty of useful books available that can instruct you on these techniques, as well as audio and video tapes. And simply making sure that you find time for yourself each and every day can go a long way to easing anxiety and pressure.

If stress is a serious problem in your life, you can take a course in stress management. The counsellors or therapists can help you work out which areas of your life are causing the most problems, and show you practical ways to reduce your stress levels or teach you stress-reduction techniques you can use at home to help you cope more effectively.

## Get some exercise

There is an unusual paradox with the relationship between migraine and exercise. On the one hand, exercise can be a trigger factor for migraine because it may cause a sudden drop in your blood sugar level. On the other hand, it can relax you, reduce your stress levels, get more oxygen and sugar to the brain, reduce muscle tension and help to lessen the frequency or severity of the attacks.

The key to making the most of exercise is to avoid overdoing it. Talk to your doctor before taking up any exercise programme. Make sure that you start off slowly and gradually increase your exercise level as you become more fit. If you are prone to migraine after exercise, you might find sucking on sugar or glucose tablets or making sure you have a light carbohydrate snack before working out can help prevent any drop in your blood sugar level. And always warm up before and stretch your muscles properly before and after exercise, as physical tension can be a cause of headache and migraine.

# Managing your migraine

*Taking regular exercise can help to lessen the frequency of migraine attacks.*

*If you find that working at a computer can cause a migraine, there are various guidelines that can help prevent this.*

 **Can computer screens and flickering lights cause migraine?**

 Many sufferers have said that when they work at a computer – or even watch television for too long – they seem to get a migraine.

It's suspected there could be a couple of reasons for this. One is that staring at a screen for long periods means that you are sitting in one position, and this could lead to muscular stress and tension in the neck and shoulders, which is often a trigger for migraine. Another reason could be that the screen flickers slightly, or that the lighting in the room where you are working is flickering almost imperceptibly.

# Managing your migraine

It's thought that flickering light can cause changes in the electrical activity in the brain in those people prone to headache and migraine. And several research groups have investigated the connection between visual stimulation and migraine. Some of the groups have found that certain patterns give rise to headache, though more studies are needed to reveal the main problems.

If you work on a computer and are prone to migraine, here are some tricks that might help prevent your being affected.

First, limit your time in front of the screen. Make sure that you get up and move around every 20 or 30 minutes, and do a few muscle stretches at the same time. Simply changing

*Watching television for long periods is known to bring on a migraine in susceptible people.*

your working position may be enough to ward off an attack.

Make sure that your computer has a good-quality display and a glare filter attached. Adjust your screen for brightness until you find which suits you best. Ensure that your computer is positioned correctly to avoid glare from any source of light being reflected on the screen.

If you spend a lot of time watching television, keep the remote control handy. This way, if your screen flickers, you can easily and quickly change to another channel.

 **I suffer from migraine and also smoke. Would giving up help reduce my attacks?**

 Cigarette smoking is often blamed as a major cause of migraine. In fact studies have not been able to confirm this. Though nicotine and other chemicals in tobacco do seem to have an effect on blood circulation and blood vessels, smoking itself does not seem to cause migraine.

However, it appears that the smell of cigarette smoke, or being in a smoky environment, is more likely to cause a migraine than actually smoking itself. If you're sensitive to strong smells during a migraine, you may find that perfumes, household cleansers or even cooking food makes the headache and accompanying symptoms such as nausea or vomiting much worse.

 **My child suffers from migraines. What can I do to make this easier for her?**

 Migraines may not only be frightening for children, but painful and uncomfortable too. As well as reassuring your daughter that she will soon be fine and there is nothing seriously wrong with her, take a careful look at her diet.

Children who suffer migraine often do so because of their eating habits – primarily lack of food rather than eating the wrong foods. Growing children need to have substantial meals at regular times throughout the day, especially if they are physically active in sport. Encourage her to have three meals a day, plus snacks if needed.

Children should also have a good breakfast before heading off to school. If your child often wakes with a migraine, try giving her a light snack just before bedtime to prevent a fall in blood sugar overnight. If she tends to suffer later in the day, pack a snack such as fruit or yoghurt to have mid-morning, again to help keep blood sugar levels steady.

You should talk to your doctor or health visitor who may also have some practical advise to make the situation easier for both of you. Fortunately migraine medication is rarely needed for children unless they have frequent or severe attacks. You may find that giving your child an over-the-counter painkiller, such as paracetamol, can help. Remember: never give aspirin to children under the age of 12.

# Managing your migraine

## Helping a child with migraine

*During a migraine attack, a child will need careful reassurance.*

# Helping a child with migraine

Children usually have different migraine triggers from adult sufferers. It is more common that an attack will develop as a result of stress of some kind: for instance, physical exercise, lack of sleep, missing meals and anxiety about school.

If your child is a sufferer, try to do your best to ensure that he or she develops a routine where possible. This means having a nutritious breakfast, as missing breakfast can easily lead to migraine in children. If you notice that your child is having any problems at home or at school, try to discuss this with him or her. You may be able to find ways of relieving some of his or her stress and anxiety. Although children are notorious for not wanting to go to bed, getting enough sleep and developing good sleeping patterns are also important factors that could help prevent your child's migraine attacks.

It can be very frightening for a child to experience a migraine attack, especially if it is accompanied by an aura. He or she may fear that there is something seriously wrong. Try to explain, using simple terms, what a migraine attack is and reassure the child that he or she will come to no harm.

The child may prefer to lie quietly in a darkened room. If the pain is bad, give him or her simple painkillers such as paracetamol – never give aspirin to a child under 12. If these do not work, never even consider giving your child medicine that has been prescribed for an adult.

If your child regularly suffers from severe or disabling migraine, do talk to your doctor about the possibility of getting prescription medicine for use during an attack. Fortunately it is very rarely necessary to give children preventative medicine – that is, medicine to take in case an attack might strike. If your child suffers from vomiting or nausea, again ask your doctor about whether anti-emetics (anti-nausea drugs) would be useful in this case.

*Chapter six*

# Seeing the doctor

Even if you are certain that your attacks are due to migraine and you are managing fairly well, it is a good idea to see your doctor for a number of reasons. First your doctor will want to check that your self-diagnosis is correct – he or she will want to make sure that your symptoms are not caused by something other than migraine.

The doctor also will have a number of medications he or she can prescribe or recommend for your migraine, if you feel that you need them. And, of course, he or she will be able to offer you practical suggestions, support and advice on the best ways of managing your migraine attacks.

Seeing your doctor is especially important if you are not certain of the cause of your headaches or if they change in nature – for instance, if they become more frequent or severe, or if you change from having migraine without aura to migraine with aura. Although very few headaches are due to anything serious, such as a brain tumour, many people who suffer migraine are very frightened about their condition. So a visit to the doctor can help to reassure you that your headaches and migraine, while distressing, are not due to something more serious or life-threatening.

## Be prepared

When you first visit your doctor, it is a good idea to go prepared with as much information about your migraine symptoms as possible. This is where your attack and trigger diaries (see pages 39 and 40) will come in very handy. In addition to the diaries, you should also make a note beforehand of the various treatments you have tried, including any over-the-counter remedies, prescription medicines and even complementary therapies. This will help your doctor to work out with you which of the treatments may be best for you.

You should also note down as much information as you can about your migraine: for example, at what point in your life the headaches first started, if they have changed at all over the years and in what way. The more facts you can provide to your doctor, the easier it will be for him or her to assess your problem. It will also make it easier for the two of you to work out a treatment plan to suit your individual needs.

## Key questions to help your doctor

Before you go in to see your doctor, write down the answers to the following questions and, if you wish, take them with you. It is likely that he or she will ask for this information and it means that you have it easily to hand.

● How old were you when you had your first attack?

● How often do you get migraine?

● About how long do your attacks last?

● Have the attacks changed over time, becoming either more or less frequent or severe?

● What kinds of symptoms do you get with your migraine attack?

● Can you think of anything that usually triggers your migraines?

● (For women) Are they connected to your menstrual cycle?

● What medicines or treatments have you already tried?

● Which ones worked, and which ones provided little or no relief?

● How do the migraines affect you – for example, are you able to work through them or do you need to lie down and rest quietly?

● How do you feel between your attacks?

## *What will the doctor do?*

Because there is no diagnostic test for migraine – your doctor cannot do an X-ray or brain scan, for instance, and tell you that your symptoms are due to migraine – in most cases the doctor will come to a diagnosis by excluding other causes for your headaches.

The first step is usually to take a full medical history, which helps to give the doctor clues on which to focus during the physical examination. This means he or she may ask questions about your health and lifestyle – for example, about your diet, your exercise habits, whether or not you smoke, the type of work you do. Undoubtedly he or she will also ask about your family's health, especially with regard to

migraine. Because migraine tends to run in families, it is possible that other members of your family also have attacks. Knowledge of these help provide the doctor with clues as to whether or not migraine is your problem. So do not be alarmed if you get asked a lot of questions. All of this enables the doctor to build up a well-rounded picture of your health, instead of just focusing on your immediate symptoms.

The doctor will also perform a general physical examination. This may include checking your heart and lungs, your blood pressure and weight, and any other area that your doctor feels is necessary.

# Seeing the doctor

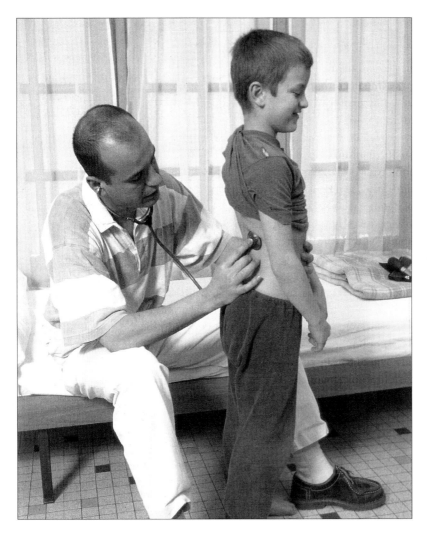

*When you first see your doctor about your migraine, he will probably carry out a general physical examination.*

In addition it is possible that your doctor will carry out a basic neurological examination to check some of your brain functions. This examination might include testing your reflexes and doing a quick check of the retina of the eye to see if there is any pressure that could indicate the presence of a growth or tumour –

which can be a cause of severe headaches.

In addition the doctor may perform some investigations to try to see if there is an underlying cause for the headaches, although these are not usually necessary. For instance, he or she may take some blood to be tested for anaemia, or may refer you for liver or kidney function tests, or even refer you for an X-ray to see if there is a problem with your cervical spine, the uppermost part of the spine which connects with the skull. This could indicate a physical cause for your headaches. Only very rarely will you be referred for specialized tests such as a brain scan. And if you are, it is to exclude other causes for your migraine.

Once your doctor has all the information, he or she will be able to decide whether or not migraine is the cause of your symptoms. And once a firm diagnosis is made, the two of you can work out a suitable treatment plan. If you have not already kept a trigger diary, your doctor can help you to identify possible causes of your attacks. This could eventually help you

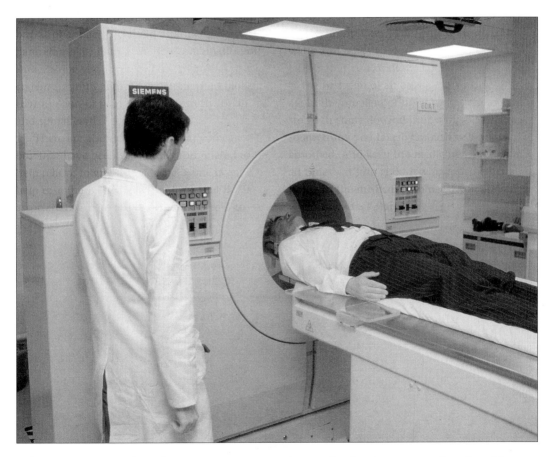

*A brain scan cannot show that your symptoms are due to migraine, but you may be referred for one to eliminate any other possible causes of your headaches.*

# Seeing the doctor

to reduce the number of migraines you suffer.

Different medications and treatments are effective for different sufferers. There is no way to tell if the first treatment is going to be the best. So it may take some time, and several visits, before the two of you have determined which type of treatment or combination of treatments most effectively eliminates or reduces your migraine attacks.

As yet, there are no firm guidelines on the best way for doctors to help patients with migraine. Different doctors will have various opinions and ways of working. Some may prefer to start on the soft and gentle medications, while others may prefer to give you something stronger.

A number of headache and migraine organizations are trying to determine whether setting up management guidelines for doctors would be useful. But because migraine varies so much between individuals, a more personalized treatment regime may be the most effective. However, until these guidelines are established, you must trust that your doctor will try to do

## Migraine clinics

You may be under the impression that a specialist migraine clinic is only for those sufferers who have very frequent or severe attacks. This is definitely not the case. A visit to a migraine clinic can be useful for anyone who has migraine, even if they suffer just the occasional attack. There is a number of reasons for this.

First the doctors and staff there specialize in migraine, unlike family doctors. They are therefore completely up to date with the latest thinking and research and may be able to answer some of your questions that your doctor could not. They may be involved in research projects or testing, so you might be in the front line of therapy and find something that works very effectively for you. And, of course, they have more time to spend with each patient, so they will be able to explain migraine fully to you and help to remove some of the fears you may have. They also have a whole host of suggestions and ideas for improving your lifestyle to assist you in reducing the severity or frequency of your attacks or help you to cope with them more effectively.

When you first visit your doctor, discuss the possibility of being referred to a migraine clinic. There is a number of these around the country. In the UK, in many cases, the treatment you receive will be available through the National Health Service. In other cases it will be considered private treatment, which you will need to pay for yourself or, if you have health insurance, may be covered by your policy.

the best he or she can for you. So do not be concerned or alarmed if you know someone else with migraine who received a different prescription or who underwent different tests. There is no true right or wrong way to treat migraine – it is a matter of discovering what works for each individual patient. And it is usually best left up to the doctor, working alongside you, to decide on the most appropriate course of action.

 **I've just started getting headaches and I'm not sure if these are due to migraine or some other condition. Is it worth a visit to my doctor?**

 Although migraines are not life-threatening, headaches, like other types of pain, can occasionally serve as a warning signal of more serious disorders. For instance, headaches can be caused by infections such as meningitis or sinusitis, and in very rare instances – if

accompanied by other symptoms – can indicate a brain tumour or impending stroke. They can also occur after a fall or some other trauma (injury) to the head.

Migraine is a specific condition and is not just a 'bad headache'. It usually affects one side of the head only, lasts around four to 72 hours, and is accompanied by nausea and/or vomiting and a dislike of noise or bright lights.

Although not all headaches require medical attention, as you have just started getting them it's a good idea to see your doctor. An expert medical opinion will help exclude the possibility of your headaches being caused by something more serious, and can also help you to get a diagnosis on the cause.

Some headaches should always be investigated, for instance, if:
● the headache is sudden and severe;
● it is associated with convulsions or seizures;
● you lose consciousness or become confused;
● you also have pain in the eye or ear;
● it is associated with a fever;
● it begins after around the age of 50 and you have previously been headache-free.

*Chapter seven*

# Medicines for migraine

There is any number of medicines available to help ease the headache pain of migraine, and to alleviate the nausea and vomiting that are common symptoms of an attack. These can range from over-the-counter painkillers you buy at the pharmacist to prescription-only medicines.

It is important to realize that there is no medicine that will cure migraine, although some will stop a migraine attack from developing. What most are designed to do is either reduce pain and symptoms during an attack, or reduce the overall frequency and severity of attacks.

It is best for you to discuss with your doctor all the possible drug options, depending on what type of relief you are looking for. Some of the drug treatment is for an acute – or immediate – attack. It is designed to be taken the minute a migraine starts and can be useful if you have infrequent attacks and you generally cope fairly well.

Other medicines are preventative and you will need to take them daily for a certain period of time to help reduce the frequency of your attacks. These are useful for people who suffer severe or frequent migraines, and who find that they are not able to manage on their own. If you are not prepared to take medicine on a daily basis, let your doctor know. There is little point in working out a treatment plan that includes daily preventative medicine if you are unwilling to continue with this type of treatment.

## Acute treatments

Medicines you take only during an attack can include painkillers you buy at a pharmacy or supermarket, as well as specific treatments for migraine available only on prescription.

## Over-the-counter painkillers

Over-the-counter (OTC) drugs usually contain aspirin, paracetamol or ibuprofen. Sometimes they are combined with small doses of other drugs, such as codeine, to make them more powerful. And there are now OTC painkillers which have been developed specifically to treat migraine.

The type of OTC painkiller you choose can depend on a number of factors, including your overall health and whether you are taking any other medicines. For example, aspirin should be avoided by pregnant women and by people suffering from bleeding disorders or peptic ulcers, and should never be given to children under 12. The best suggestion is to talk to your doctor or pharmacist about which painkiller would be best for you.

To get the most out of your medicine, you should take it as early in the attack as is possible. If you find that any painkiller is not effective, or not as effective as it once was, it is time to see your doctor about other options.

## Prescription drugs

When and if simple painkillers become ineffective, your doctor has a number of different medications he or she can discuss with you. Anti-emetics are usually the next line of treatment, taken together with painkillers. If this does not work, you may be recommended to try specific migraine medication. The two main drugs used to treat migraine attacks do not work as painkillers. Instead they are thought to help reduce the pain of a migraine headache by narrowing the swollen blood vessels in the head.

### Anti-emetics

Anti-emetics, or anti-nausea drugs, help to relieve the nausea and/or vomiting that are so common with migraine attacks. Some anti-emetics available on prescription also help to reverse the stomach shut-down, or stasis, and aid the absorption of painkillers, making them more effective. They come in various forms, including tablets, soluble forms and suppositories. The suppositories are useful for sufferers who are unable to take any medicine by mouth because they cannot keep anything down, including a tablet or water.

*Side effects*
Some anti-emetic drugs can cause drowsiness, lethargy, dizziness, insomnia or diarrhoea. Most, however, have few side effects.

### Ergotamine

Ergotamine has been used successfully for over 60 years to treat migraine. It is a vaso-constrictor, and seems to help stop migraine attacks by narrowing the dilated blood vessels. You can obtain this drug in a number of different forms, including tablets and suppositories. There is also a tablet form that is placed under the tongue and absorbed into the bloodstream, and an inhaler for rapid relief of migraine.

*Side effects*
Ergotamine can cause side effects, especially because it affects not only the blood vessels in the brain but those all round the body too. So if you notice any tingling, numbness or

# Medicines for migraine

coldness in fingers and toes, stop taking ergotamine and discuss the problem with your doctor: it could be the result of the drug · causing overconstriction in other blood vessels. You may need to take a lower dose or stop the drug altogether. Other possible side effects include nausea, vomiting and drowsiness, which are similar to the symptoms of migraine itself. It can be difficult to determine whether the symptoms are caused by the attack or by the drug.

## Sumatriptan

Sumatriptan is a newer drug that was developed specifically for the treatment of migraine. In some ways it works in a similar fashion to ergotamine, by reducing the size of the swollen blood vessels. But in most people it affects only the cranial blood vessels – those in the brain – rather than blood vessels throughout the body. And this is what makes it such a breakthrough. Sumatriptan is available in tablet and self-injection form.

*Side effects*

There are side effects that can occur with sumatriptan, including fluttering or tightness in the chest or throat. Rarely, swelling or a rash may develop, all of which can indicate an allergic reaction to the medicine. As with ergotamine, you may notice tiredness or dizziness and nausea or vomiting, which can be difficult to distinguish from your migraine symptoms.

## NSAIDS

NSAIDs (non-steroidal anti-inflammatory drugs) are often taken by people who suffer from chronic pain due to arthritis. They work by inhibiting the production of prostaglandins, the chemicals that help to pass on pain signals to the brain and also inflame surrounding tissue.

*Side effects*

Side effects that are common with this type of drug include nausea, vomiting, heartburn and indigestion. It can also cause gastrointestinal bleeding.

# *Preventative treatment*

If you have frequent or severe migraines which interfere with your work and social life, your doctor may suggest that you consider a medication you take daily to help prevent the attacks, rather than something that is useful only once an attack has started. This type of drug helps you to break the cycle of migraine attacks, so that they can be kept under control. They are not designed to be an alternative to

treating an acute attack. But when a migraine does strike, it may be less severe and your usual medication may prove to keep it under control or bearable.

Preventative drugs have not specifically been designed to treat migraine. Instead they are more commonly used for other conditions such as high blood pressure or depression. But when being used by sufferers of these other

*If your migraines are severe enough to interfere seriously with your work, your doctor may suggest a preventative medication.*

# Medicines for migraine

conditions who also suffer from migraine, they were found to help keep the migraine under control too.

None of these drugs will take effect immediately, so you must be willing to give the treatment time to work. Many sufferers stop taking their medication before it has been given enough of a chance. Ask your doctor how long it will be before you should start to notice an improvement. If your migraines do not improve within this time, go back to see your doctor. It may be that you need a different dosage, or you may need a different treatment altogether.

You should also ask your doctor what side effects, if any, you might expect with treatment. Ask too whether any of these side effects are serious, and if there are ways to minimize the risk of suffering from them.

## Beta blockers

Beta blockers are drugs that are most commonly used to treat hypertension, or high blood pressure. They work by their effects on the blood vessels. Beta blockers seem to control the process by which blood vessels close and then open.

### Side effects

You may notice mild dizziness or a stomach upset when taking beta blockers. If you find the discomfort difficult to cope with, it is important that you discuss this with your doctor. You may also find that you experience tiredness during the day but suffer insomnia at night with vivid dreams during periods of sleep.

## Anti-depressants

Anti-depressants are just what they sound – they are medication to help relieve depression. The reason why some types of anti-depressant may be useful for migraine is that they affect the production of serotonin (see page 25) in the brain, which is thought to have an effect on mood. And they are useful for migraine even if you do not suffer from depression. There are different types of anti-depressants, but the ones most often prescribed for migraine sufferers are the tricyclics. They are usually given in lower doses than those used to treat depression.

### Side effects

The most common side effects with anti-depressants include dry mouth, constipation, blurred vision and dizziness. These often settle down within a few days or weeks of treatment.

## 5-HT antagonists

One drug, called pizotifen, works as a 5-HT antagonist. This means that it is able to work against, or block, the effects of 5-HT (or seratonin) when it is released into the body. And like other preventative drugs it seems to help raise your threshold to migraine triggers, so in effect it may take more than one trigger, or a greater exposure to trigger factors, before you succumb to a migraine attack. It comes in tablet and liquid form.

### Side effects

Pizotifen commonly causes an increased appetite which leads to weight gain. Drowsiness, dry mouth and occasionally dizziness and nausea can also occur.

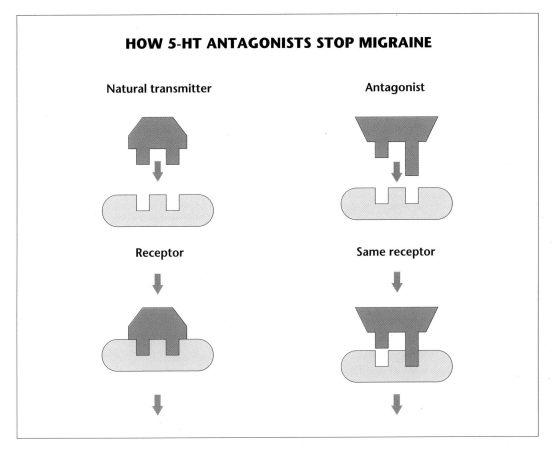

## HOW 5-HT ANTAGONISTS STOP MIGRAINE

**Natural transmitter**  **Antagonist**

**Receptor**  **Same receptor**

*The neurotransmitter 5-HT (serotonin) and its receptors on various cells work like a lock and key. When 5-HT comes into contact with the receptor, it is able to cause biochemical changes within the body. 5-HT antagonists, however, do not fit the receptor and so are unable to produce a response.*

**Can certain medications lead to migraine?**

Many drugs, both prescription and over-the-counter types, have side-effects ranging from the very mild to the more serious. Certain non-headache medications may have an influence on migraine and may actually cause or worsen it, although few studies have been done on specific drugs.

Many medications for heart conditions or high blood pressure have an effect on the

# Medicines for migraine

blood vessels, so it is possible – though not necessarily probable – that they may cause headache or worsen migraine if you are already susceptible. And in rare instances diuretics, given to prevent fluid retention, have been known to worsen migraine attacks.

When you are being given a prescription or choosing a medicine from the pharmacy, the best advice is to always mention to your doctor or pharmacist that you suffer from migraine. Ask if the medicine you are planning to take will have any effect on your condition. And if you do notice a possible link between starting your medicine and a change in your migraines, let your doctor know. It may be pure coincidence, or it may be that you need to switch to some other formulation of the drug.

## Tips on taking your medicine

● Follow the instructions carefully, and ask your pharmacist about any special advice you should have: for instance, should you take the tablets with meals or avoid alcohol?

● Be sure to tell your doctor if you are taking any other medicines, including the contraceptive pill, vitamin and mineral supplements, or herbal remedies.

● If you are pregnant or think you could be pregnant, always tell your doctor.

● Always take the correct dose. If the medicine does not appear to be working, more is not necessarily better.

● Some of the medicines may cause drowsiness, especially if you are also drinking alcohol. Ask if this is common with your medication, and avoid driving or using heavy machinery while taking it.

● Let your doctor or pharmacist know if you suffer any symptoms or side effects you suspect might be due to the medication. Find out if it is safe to continue taking the medicine or if you should stop immediately.

● Keep the medicine with you at all times rather than stored at home in the medicine cabinet. You may need it when you are out of the house, and most medicines for acute attacks are most effective if you take them just as soon as you notice the first signs of a migraine.

● In most cases tablets taken before a meal are more quickly absorbed than those taken afterwards.

● If your medicine does not appear to be working, see your doctor to discuss other options.

**I don't want to take strong medicines for my migraine. Is there anything available over the counter that is effective?**

 Many migraine sufferers forget about the power of simple analgesics (over-the-counter painkillers). There is a number that can be very useful for migraine. Most you can buy at pharmacists contain aspirin, paracetamol or ibuprofen, or a combination of these. Some also include small quantities of codeine, a mild narcotic which helps to block transmission of pain signals within the brain and spinal cord.

There are also medications that you can buy that have been specifically formulated to help relieve migraine headache. Some even help ease the nausea and vomiting that is associated with an attack. And one is said to help reverse the dilation of blood vessels in the brain, which can be one of the causes of a migraine headache.

Before choosing, ask your pharmacist for advice on selecting the one appropriate for you. Be sure to let him or her know if you are pregnant or taking any other medication, or if you suffer from any other medical condition.

To get the best out of your painkiller, buy a soluble form if available. This is dissolved in water and tends to work more quickly than tablets that you swallow. Take the medication at the first sign of an attack. This helps to avoid the problem of non-absorption, as your stomach shuts down during a migraine attack, so anything you take by mouth will not be absorbed. And keep the medicine with you at all times – it's no good having a painkiller at home in the medicine cabinet if you are out when the attack starts.

## Chapter eight

# Complementary therapies

One of the difficulties with chronic conditions such as migraine is that it can wear you down. You may feel unwell for a day or a few days before an attack and find that it can take you some time to recover afterwards. And if you suffer frequent attacks, see your doctor about them and/or take preventative medication for your migraines, you may find that this all takes its toll. Being a migraine sufferer can sap your energy and you can begin to see yourself as an unhealthy person rather than as a well person who happens to suffer from migraine.

One way to deal with this is to look for complementary therapies that, although they will not 'cure' your migraine, could help you to feel better about yourself. What is more, many complementary therapies have been used for easing headache and migraine very successfully.

## Effective additional treatment

In the past many medical experts scoffed at complementary therapies. These orthodox doctors frequently dismissed the role they can play in helping patients to feel better. But some studies have shown that complementary therapies can be effective, and many patients report that their condition improves as a result of treatment. A number of these therapies is especially good in helping to treat conditions which are often stress-related, such as migraine.

However, as their name implies, they are intended to be used to complement or work alongside any medical treatment or drugs that you are taking. You should never stop taking any medication without discussing it with your doctor first. This is absolutely crucial, and any therapists who tell you to stop taking the tablets are not doing their job properly.

It is also important that you realize that, like conventional medication, complementary therapy will not work for everyone. You may know someone whose migraine improved dramatically after acupuncture, for example, yet meet others who found no relief whatsoever. You may need to try more than one therapy before you find one that helps. And you should also be aware that these therapies are not a quick fix – it may take some time and a number of sessions before you experience any relief.

## Finding a therapist

As yet many areas of complementary health are not regulated by the Government. This means that for some therapies there is any number of organizations and bodies which provide training and qualifications. In some instances almost anyone can set up shop as a complementary therapist without undergoing specialist training. This is why you should take some time to find a qualified practitioner. The best course of action is to contact one of organizations listed at the back of this book. They will usually provide free, or for a nominal charge, a list of their practising members in your area.

When you get in touch with an organization, do not be afraid to ask questions about what type of training its members undergo, how long this training lasts, and what type of insurance the members carry. The organization will also usually be able to provide detailed information about the therapy itself, whether it would be useful in the treatment of migraine, what the therapy involves, and what you can expect from treatment.

Once you have found a practitioner and made an appointment, again do not be afraid to ask questions. You should find out a little more about his or her personal qualifications, how long he or she has been practising and what training he or she has undergone. And again, do not forget to ask if the practitioner is insured to carry out this type of therapy.

One of the most important aspects of your treatment is to find a therapist that you trust and feel comfortable with. Complementary therapists often spend as much as an hour or more with each patient. They will be asking a lot of detailed questions about your medical and personal history, so to establish a good working relationship you must be willing to confide in them, just as you would in a medical doctor.

*Being a migraine sufferer can sap your energy, but complementary therapies could help you to feel better about yourself.*

# Complementary therapies

## What will it cost?

Because of the increased interest in complementary therapy, and the admission that it can and does work for some people, your chosen therapy may be available on the National Health Service (NHS) in the UK. The most common ones provided for in this way include acupuncture, homoeopathy, chiropractic and osteopathy. But do not give up hope if the therapy you wish to try is not on the list. Your doctor can refer you for treatment if he or she feels it would be worthwhile, so do ask. Doctors sometimes even have a complementary therapist connected to their practice, or indeed have been trained themselves. And a number of private health companies also will pay for treatment with a complementary therapist, both in the UK and USA, depending on what the treatment is for.

If you cannot get treatment on the NHS or through health insurance, you will be paying for treatment out of your own pocket. This is why you should try to get some idea of what your treatment will cost before you make a large financial commitment.

When you have located a therapist, or when you initially contact one of the registering organizations, you should also ask how much each treatment or session will cost, and try to get a rough idea of how much an entire course, if necessary, will cost you. You may think trying complementary therapy would be helpful, only to find out that it may be prohibitively expensive for you. In many cases therapists will not be able to tell you a great deal more than how much each session costs initially. Once you have had an assessment and initial treatment, they will be better placed to give you an idea of how many treatments you will need, and how long all this is likely to take.

## The initial treatment

At a first appointment therapists will, in most cases, take a detailed medical history. They will ask you about your symptoms, about what treatments you have already tried and how successful they were. They will also ask detailed questions about your general health and that of your family – many of the same questions a medical doctor would ask.

Complementary therapists tend to look at you as a whole person, and not just your individual symptoms. So gaining an understanding about your health in general is very important to the treatment they carry out. And, depending on the therapist, they may carry out blood or urine tests, take X-rays, or do a physical examination.

Once they have built up a picture of your overall health, they are in the position of being able to put together a treatment plan that is suitable for you. Therapists may give you advice about reducing your stress levels or changing your diet, or talk to you about more personal situations that are taking place in your life. All of this is normal, so do not be alarmed if they seem to be straying from the source of your trouble – your migraine.

Again, like most orthodox treatments, some complementary therapies will take a while to bring about any change or benefit. You should discuss with your therapist how many sessions you might need, what side effects you might encounter and how long it should be before you notice any improvement.

So if you do not find that you are better after the first treatment, do not give up. It is worth persevering for a while. At the same time, however, do not break the bank doing it. It simply could be that this therapy, which possibly worked for someone you know, is just not suitable for you.

## Protecting yourself

Although there is no guarantee that a complementary therapy will work for you, one way to get the best from your treatment is to make sure you find a qualified and reputable practitioner.

● Tell your doctor that you are planning to see a complementary therapist. The doctor may be able to offer treatment on the NHS, or even in his or her own surgery.

● If NHS treatment is not possible, ask your doctor if he or she is familiar with any practitioners in your area. Alternatively ask friends if they have been satisfied with a therapist they have visited.

● Contact the governing body or relevant organization for your chosen therapy. Most will provide lists of registered practitioners in your area. Find out what training and qualifications are required.

● Once you have made an appointment, ask the therapist how much each session might cost, what you can expect, and how long it should be before you may notice any results. Ask also if they are insured to carry out this treatment.

● Realize that no treatment will be a panacea for all ills. Ask your therapist to be specific regarding what he or she can and cannot do.

● Avoid practitioners who claim to be able to cure your illness, or that their treatment is good for almost every ailment. Remember that no responsible practitioner would tell you to stop taking any medication without your doctor's approval or to forego medical treatment.

● Ask the therapist to keep your doctor informed of your treatment.

● Make sure that you feel comfortable with your therapist, as the success of your treatment depends to a great extent upon this relationship.

# Complementary therapies

## Suitable complementary therapies for migraine

Although there are many complementary therapies available, the following is a brief outline of the ones most commonly used to help migraine.

### Acupuncture

Acupuncture is a traditional form of Chinese medicine. Treatment involves inserting needles or applying pressure to specific points along the body's meridian system – invisible channels lying beneath the skin that are said to be the flow of life energy. This energy or life force is called *Qi* in traditional Chinese medicine.

A wide range of ailments and conditions is said to occur when you have an imbalance or blockage of energy along these meridians. The aim of acupuncture is to help unblock and rebalance your own personal energy flow.

Even though a number of studies has been carried out to try to discover how and why acupuncture seems to work, there are no firm answers as yet. In general the Western view of acupuncture is that it in some way helps release endorphins, the body's natural painkillers.

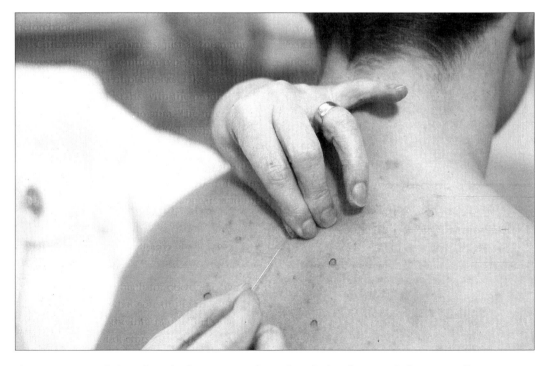

*Acupuncture can help reduce the frequency and severity of migraine attacks in some sufferers.*

This is why it seems to be so successful at helping to control pain, including that of migraine. A course of treatments can be used to reduce the frequency and severity of attacks, or you can have treatment during an attack to try to help control the immediate pain.

The needles used during acupuncture are extremely fine, and they are usually either disposable or sterilized, so you are at no risk of infection. The needles do not cause pain or bleeding, though many people who have had acupuncture treatment say they feel a slight tingling sensation afterwards.

## Aromatherapy

Aromatherapy involves treatment using essential oils which have been distilled from plants and flowers. It is known that smell is a very powerful sense, and it can affect our brain, our moods and ultimately our health.

The essential oils can work in a number of different ways. First the inhaled scent travels up through the nose and reaches the brain, where it can affect the nervous system. When used in a massage or a bath, some of the molecules of the oils are absorbed into the bloodstream, so entering the circulatory system. Again this eventually ends up in the centres of the brain.

Trials carried out on the effects of aromatherapy have shown that certain oils may help us to sleep better, may relieve pain and headache, and also may help ease depression. Now a number of nurses and other clinicians in orthodox medicine are practising aromatherapy treatment, often using it in hospitals or hospices to ease the pain of cancer patients.

You can buy essential oils from health-food shops and by mail order. But you must use them carefully as some are quite powerful. And some of the oils are not suitable if you are pregnant or breastfeeding or if you have other medical conditions besides your migraine.

The best course of action is to visit a qualified aromatherapist. The therapist will be able to help determine which oils or combination of oils will be best for you, will talk to you about your condition and will offer practical support and advice.

## Try it yourself: aromatherapy

The essential oils often have very specific effects on the body. You may find that using ginger or peppermint oil can help reduce the feeling of nausea you get during a migraine attack, as they are known to aid digestion. Lavender oil is said to be good for easing headaches, including migraine. One way to use it is to sprinkle a few drops on a tissue and inhale at regular intervals. Another is to rub a tiny amount on to your temples. Be careful not to use too much oil and do not get the oil into your eyes.

# Complementary therapies

## Chiropractic medicine

Chiropractic medicine is a type of manipulative therapy, similar to osteopathy. It is based on the fact that the human body is a machine that has a mechanical structure. If this structure, especially the spine, gets damaged, distorted or irritated, the result can be acute or nagging pain. This pain can be anywhere, not just in the back or neck.

Chiropractors have been specially trained to look for spinal nerve stress, often using X-rays. Once this has been identified, the therapist can manipulate the affected area to correct the condition and relieve the stress so that the body can restore itself to normal. And a number of studies have shown that chiropractic treatment is useful for certain types of headache, including migraine if it is caused by tension, stress or a misalignment in the spine.

You may be able to get chiropractic treatment through the NHS, if your doctor is willing to refer you, or through private health insurance. Otherwise you are free to contact a qualified chiropractor on your own, without a referral. If your condition will not be helped by treatment, the therapist will let you know and refer you elsewhere if necessary.

## Herbal medicine

Herbal medicine is probably one of the oldest forms of medicine – it has been used for thousands of years. Many of the drugs and medicines we have today are a result of synthesizing traditional herbal remedies.

As with most other complementary therapies, herbalism seeks to restore your body's ability to heal itself. Therapists will generally not treat a symptom in isolation, so they may ask you a number of questions about your health and lifestyle. Traditional Chinese herbalists will often look at your tongue, as they believe that the tongue is a good barometer of your health. Both Western and Chinese herbalists may also give you a simple physical examination.

Once they have made a diagnosis, they will prescribe you the appropriate remedy along with careful instructions on how to take it properly. Some herbalists can dispense the herbs on the spot, while with others you may be required to get them from someone else. In most cases you will need to go back for another appointment soon after the first, so your herbalist can determine whether you are improving or whether the remedy needs adjusting.

## Homoeopathy

Homoeopathy is based on the principle that 'like is cured by like'. So a substance that causes certain symptoms in a healthy person can be used to cure someone else who has developed similar symptoms as a result of disease.

Homoeopathy, like many other forms of complementary therapy, does not try to suppress or treat symptoms. It is very individual, and designed to reveal the underlying cause of the symptoms and then treat this. You will not, for instance, find a homoeopathic 'migraine remedy'. Instead the homoeopath will try to build up a picture of you and your health, including your mental and emotional wellbeing. From this he or she will decide on a remedy that is suitable for you.

## Try it yourself: feverfew

A number of studies have shown that the herb feverfew can reduce the frequency and severity of migraine attacks. It also seems to help with other symptoms of migraine such as nausea or vomiting.

Although it has been used for centuries to relieve migraine, only recently have studies been able to show how it works. It is now thought that feverfew contains a natural chemical called parthenolide. This may work by inhibiting the release of serotonin from the platelets (see page 25), helping to keep blood flow steady and regular.

Feverfew is not designed to bring relief during an acute attack. Instead it is meant to be taken over a period of time to help lessen the attacks. Most sufferers say that you should allow at least six weeks before any beneficial results are likely to be noticed. But you do not need to take it forever. A course of feverfew lasting up to three months could help reduce the number of attacks you have, or keep you migraine-free, for quite a long period of time.

Although you can grow and dry feverfew yourself, most people find it much easier and more convenient to take tablets. You can buy feverfew at supermarkets, chemists and health-food shops. It is important that the brand you buy contains at least 0.2 per cent of the active ingredient parthenolide, so read the label carefully.

Feverfew can cause side effects, including mouth ulcers, stomach pain and occasionally swollen lips. You should not take it if you are pregnant or breastfeeding. If you decide to try feverfew, it is a good idea to discuss it first with your doctor, especially if you are taking any other medication, even if it is not for migraine.

Homoeopathic remedies are safe, as the substances are extremely diluted. They are also suitable for children. As yet, no one is really sure how or why homoeopathy works. It is one of the therapies available on the NHS, and there is a number of NHS homoeopathic hospitals around the UK. If you wish to try it, it is worth asking your doctor for a referral to one of these specialist institutions rather than trying to treat yourself with a homoeopathic remedy bought from the chemist.

## Meditation

There are various different schools of meditation, the best known of which is probably transcendental meditation. Several clinical trials and studies have shown that meditation can help to relieve stress, lower your blood pressure, reduce headaches and migraine and ease other stress-related problems.

Although you do not need to take a course or see a therapist to learn how to meditate, it is probably best to be taught by experts to be

# Complementary therapies

*Reducing the level of stress in your life is likely to reduce the number of migraine attacks you have.*

certain that you are doing it properly. This will ensure that you are getting the most benefit from meditation. In the case of some types of meditation you need to meditate only when you feel it is necessary. With transcendental meditation it is recommended that you meditate for 20 minutes twice a day to gain the most benefit.

## Osteopathy

Osteopathy is similar to chiropractic medicine. It is a manipulative therapy concerned with structural and mechanical problems in the body. Many osteopaths find that patients who suffer frequent headaches or migraine also have neck and shoulder stiffness, or experience problems with or a misalignment of the upper part of the spine or the cranial (skull) bones. A specific type of treatment, known as cranial osteopathy, has been shown to be useful for some sufferers of migraine.

The therapist will usually take a detailed history, and may also use X-rays to determine the cause of the problem. Treatment may involve manipulation, soft tissue massage, and repetitive stretching to ease tense and contracted muscles.

## Reflexology

According to reflexologists, your organs and parts of your body are reflected in your feet. By pressing and massaging the soles and toes they release blocked energy and your body's natural ability to heal itself is restored. Reflexology is claimed to help a number of stress-related conditions, including migraine.

Treatment lasts around an hour. The practitioner will use his or her hands and thumbs to apply pressure to various parts of the feet. You should feel relaxed after treatment, though some people find that their feet are a little sore the day afterwards.

## Shiatsu

Shiatsu is a Japanese term meaning 'finger pressure'. The therapy is a combination of massage, pressure on acupuncture points, and some manipulation. The practitioner will use the fingers, thumbs, elbows, knees and even feet to apply pressure on the specific points. This pressure is designed to release blocked energy from the meridians, or energy channels, which are the same energy channels used in acupuncture.

Shiatsu is said to help stimulate circulation and the flow of lymphatic fluid. This helps to release toxins and waste products that have built up in the muscles, easing tension and encouraging relaxation. You are fully clothed when having a Shiatsu treatment, and you should feel relaxed and calm after a session.

## Yoga

Yoga has been practised for over 3,000 years. It uses exercise positions, called asanas, and breathing techniques. By combining the two, yoga has been shown to help with relaxation and stress reduction.

Although a number of trials have shown yoga's benefits for other conditions, as yet there have been no major studies investigating its effect on migraine. However, many sufferers have taken up yoga and found that it helps, especially for relaxation and stress reduction. When practised regularly, yoga does help lower stress levels, which in turn can be beneficial if you suffer regular migraines. And the relaxation and breathing exercises might prove useful during an attack. Yoga is also excellent exercise in its own right and helps to improve your strength and flexibility.

Yoga has become extremely popular in recent years. As a result you may find a class run at your local leisure or sports centre or as part of an adult education programme. You can obtain information about practitioners and teachers working in the area where you live from the British Wheel of Yoga (see page 78 for the address). There are also yoga video cassettes available, which allow you to practise at home.

# Complementary therapies

*Practised regularly, yoga can benefit people who suffer from migraine.*

 **I've heard about special head bands that can help with migraine and headaches. Are these effective?**

 These bands are based on the principles of acupressure. By applying pressure to specific acupressure points on the head and temples they are said to help ease

migraine and headache. One study published in the scientific journal *Headache* tested the effectiveness of head bands. The results showed that the bands reduced the severity of pain in 23 migraine sufferers over a total of 69 headaches. Many of the patients kept using the method, often alongside other therapies, during a six-month follow-up period. If you're looking for a drug-free method to ease your migraine, it may be worth trying a head band.

*Although there is as yet no cure for migraine, there is a wide variety of treatments available to help you keep it under control – it needn't mar your enjoyment of life.*

# Useful addresses

The following organizations offer help and support to migraine sufferers as well as funding research into migraine. They publish a wide range of material, including leaflets and booklets, newsletters and fact sheets. If you write for information, please enclose a large, stamped, self-addressed envelope.

## UK

**British Migraine Association**
178a High Road
Byfleet
West Byfleet
Surrey KT14 7ED

**The Migraine Trust**
45 Great Ormond Street
London WC1N 3HZ
Tel: 0171 831 4818

For information about complementary therapies and practitioners in your area send a large, stamped, self-addressed envelope to the relevant organization(s):

*Acupuncture:*
**The British Acupuncture Council**
Park House
206–208 Latimer Road
London W10 6RE

*Aromatherapy:*
**Aromatherapy Organisations Council**
3 Latymer Close
Braybrooke
Market Harborough
Leicester LE16 8LN

*Chiropractic:*
**British Chiropractic Association**
29 Whitley Street
Reading
Berkshire RG2 0EG

*Herbal medicine:*
**National Institute of Medical Herbalists**
56 Longbrook Street
Exeter
Devon EX4 6AH

*Homoeopathy:*
**British Homoeopathic Association**
27a Devonshire Street
London W1N 1RJ

*Osteopathy:*
**Osteopathic Information Service**
PO Box 2074
Reading
Berkshire RG1 4YR

**Cranial Osteopathic Association**
478 Baker Street
Enfield
Middlesex EN1 3QS

*Reflexology:*
**Association of Reflexologists**
27 Old Gloucester Street
London WC1N 3XX

*Shiatsu:*
**Shiatsu Society**
31 Pullman Lane
Godalming
Surrey GU7 1XY

*Stress management:*
**Relaxation for Living**
12 New Street
Chipping Norton
Oxfordshire OX7 5LJ

*Yoga:*
**British Wheel of Yoga**
1 Hamilton Place
Boston Road
Sleaford
Lincolnshire
NG34 7ES

**Yoga Therapy Centre**
60 Great Ormond Street
London WC1N 3HR

**USA**

**American Council for Headache Education (ACHE)**
875 Kings Highway
Suite 200
Woodbury
New Jersey 08096

**National Headache Foundation (NHF)**
5252 North Western
Avenue
Chicago
Illinois 60625

**National Institute of Neurological Disorders and Stroke**
National Institutes of Health
Building 31
31 Center Drive
MSC 2540
Bethesda
Maryland 20892–2540

**Australia**

**The Migraine Society of Australia**
PO Box 2504
Kent Town Centre
South Australia 5071

# Index